AMULETS
OF ANCIENT EGYPT

AMULETS OF ANCIENT EGYPT

Carol Andrews

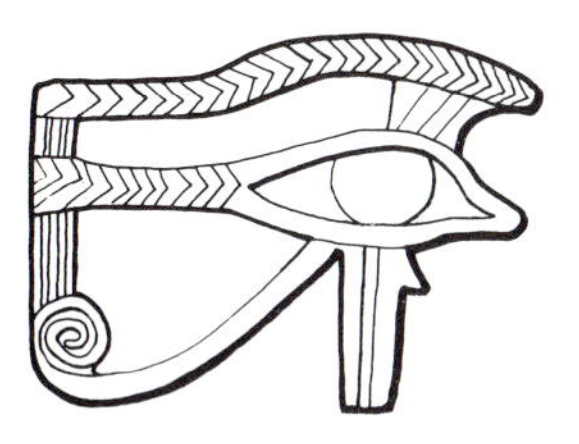

University of Texas Press

Front cover: TOP (a) Glazed-composition winged funerary scarab with holes for attachment to mummy wrappings and a flat underside. W. 11.8 cm, Saite. LEFT (b) Red jasper *tit* amulet, sacred to Isis. NK. RIGHT (c) Green jasper human-headed heart scarab in a gold mount inscribed with Chapter 30B of the *Book of the Dead* for King Sobkemsaf II of the 17th Dynasty, *c.* 1590 BC. BOTTOM (d) Polychrome glazed-composition *wedjat*-eye, the 'sound' eye of Horus, with rows of seated frontal cats. W. 8.8 cm, TIP.

Back cover: FROM LEFT TO RIGHT (a) Glazed-composition lion-headed goddess wearing a uraeus and carrying a papyrus sceptre. H. 10.5 cm, TIP. (b) Glazed-composition flat-backed plaque with high relief figures of Isis, Horus-the-Child and Nephthys. Saite. (c) Rock crystal Thoeris, carved in the round, resting on a *sa* amulet. NK.

Frontispiece: Pale green glazed-composition ibis-headed walking Thoth, scribe of the gods and inventor of writing. H. 12.3 cm, TIP to Saite Period.

Published by British Museum Press

First University of Texas Press edition, 1994
ISBN 0-292-70464-X
Library of Congress Catalog Card Number 94-60076

Designed by Behram Kapadia

Printed and bound in Great Britain by The Bath Press, Avon

Acknowledgements

Most of the illustrations are the work of Peter Hayman, and the remainder are by Janet Watt, both of the British Museum Photographic Service. The line drawings on pages 50 and 52 were produced by Mrs Christine Barratt, Graphics Officer, and those on pages 3 and 6 by Richard Parkinson, Curator, both in the Museum's Department of Egyptian Antiquities.

Abbreviations

ED	Early Dynastic Period
FIP	First Intermediate Period
G-R	Graeco-Roman Period
LD	Late Dynastic Period
LP	Late Period
MK	Middle Kingdom
NK	New Kingdom
OK	Old Kingdom
SIP	Second Intermediate Period
TIP	Third Intermediate Period

Contents

I

A Short Introduction to Egyptian Amulets

An amulet, talisman or charm is a personal ornament which, because of its shape, the material from which it is made, or even just its colour, is believed to endow its wearer by magical means with certain powers or capabilities. At the very least it should afford some kind of magical protection, a concept confirmed by the fact that three of the four Egyptian words translated as 'amulet', namely *mkt* (meket), *nht* (nehet) and *s3* (sa) come primarily from verbs meaning 'to guard' or 'to protect'. The fourth, *wḏ3* (wedja), has the same sound as the word meaning 'well-being'. For the ancient Egyptians amulets and jewellery incorporating amuletic forms were an essential adornment, especially as part of the funerary equipment for the dead, but also in the costume of the living. Moreover, many of the amulets and pieces of amuletic jewellery worn in life for their magical properties could be taken to the tomb for use in the life after death. Funerary amulets, however, and prescribed funerary jewellery which was purely amuletic in function, were made expressly for setting on the wrapped mummy on the day of burial to provide aid and protection on the fraught journey to the Other World and ease in the Afterlife.

Ancient Egyptian texts give information on the appearance and uses of amulets. In particular, certain funerary amulets are the subject of chapters in the *Book of the Dead*, a repertoire of nearly 200 spells or chapters written on papyrus and illustrated with vignettes which were intended to help the dead pass through the perils of the Underworld and reach heaven. Indeed, *Books of the Dead* themselves qualify for the term funerary amulet since a copy was placed in the burial chamber either on the mummy itself, inside the coffin or within a special compartment in a Ptah-Sokaris-Osiris figure or in the plinth on which it stood. In funerary papyri the amulets in question are illustrated in the accompanying vignette, the material from which they are to be made is specified and the spell to be recited over them, together with the desired result, forms the relevant chapter.

Although *Book of the Dead* papyri do not predate the New Kingdom, many of their spells are first found in the Middle Kingdom *Coffin Texts* which were themselves largely based on the so-called *Pyramid Texts* inscribed inside Old Kingdom pyramids from the reign of Wenis onwards (*c.* 2350 BC). Some of the spells for prescribed amulets which occur in these earlier texts were not incorporated into the *Book of the Dead*, but examples of the amulets in question have themselves survived. Such is the case for that in the form of a lion's forepart prescribed by *Coffin Text* 83: examples of First Intermediate Period date are known.

A few of the spells in the *Coffin Texts* and the *Book of the Dead* were to be recited not over an actual amuletic form but over a representation drawn on the bandages which wrapped the mummy, thus rendering the bandaging itself amuletic. It was sometimes the practice, too, in magico-medical texts of the New Kingdom and later that the spell should be recited over various amuletic images painted or drawn on linen which was then set on the relevant part of the sufferer's body. Indeed, occasionally it was

1 The Dendera amulets list, a relief representation as it appears today of 104 amulets to be set within the wrappings of the mummy, depicted on the thickness of a doorway in the western Osiris complex on the roof of the temple of Hathor at Dendera. Ptolemaic.

required that the drawing be made directly on to the patient's hand and subsequently licked off so that the potency of the image and the words pass into his body together. Most often, though, remedies involved the recitation of a spell over an actual amulet.

A well-known list of amulets is depicted on the thickness of a doorway in the complex of rooms dedicated to Osiris on the roof of the Ptolemaic temple of the goddess Hathor at Dendera. Far more informative, however, is the detailed contemporary list of amulets on the verso of a funerary papyrus, known as the MacGregor Papyrus, in which each is represented pictorially and named. Another source is a select group of amulets depicted on a wooden tablet of New Kingdom date in Berlin; of particular use is the listing of the materials from which they are made. Sometimes, too, Late Dynastic funerary papyri end with a depiction of dozens of amulets positioned in such a way that they can only reflect how they would have been placed on the mummy.

Undoubtedly the positioning of an amulet on the body must originally have had a special significance; certainly the location of the prescribed funerary amulets was always laid down. However, when mummies were first unwrapped, such information was not always recorded carefully or was even ignored. Now, though,

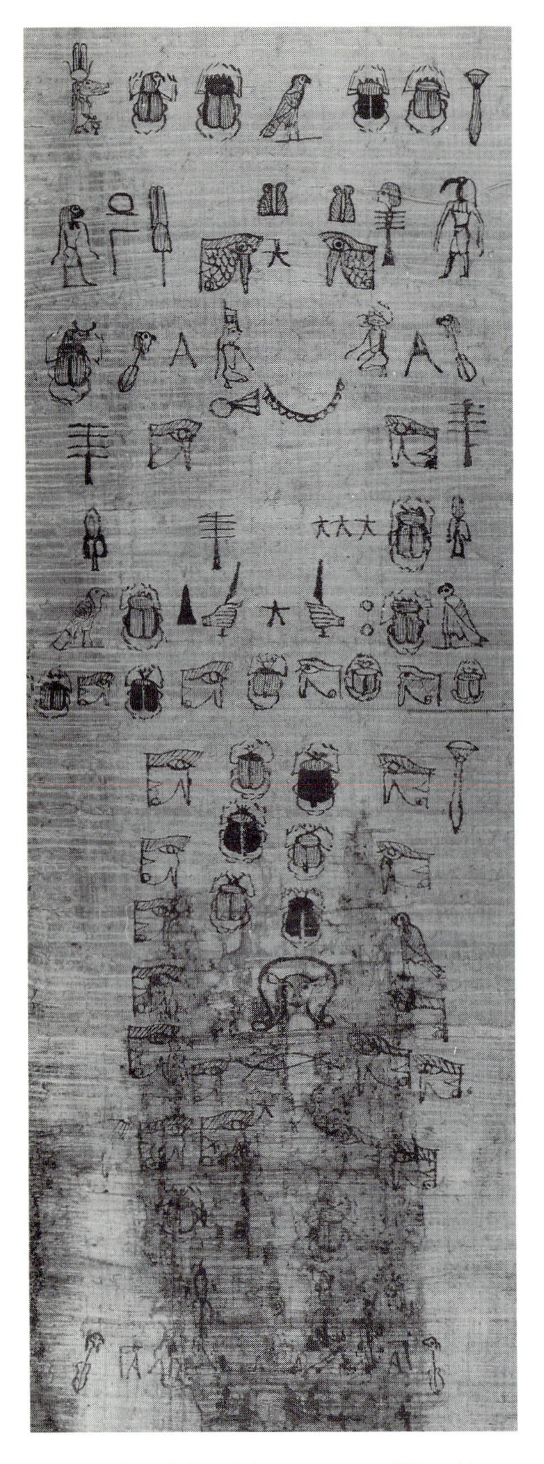

2 The last sheet of a hieratic funerary papyrus of Men with a schematic plan of the position of amulets on a contemporary mummy. Ptolemaic.

the X-raying of wrapped bodies and re-examination of evidence are providing more and more details. Although the majority of mummies examined in this way date to the last millennium BC and in particular to the last few centuries BC, it has been possible to determine that from the New Kingdom until the Ptolemaic Period the positioning of amulets on the body does appear to follow a certain pattern and it was only after this time that they came to be scattered almost randomly.

Some rare examples of original stringing have survived which suggest that, in the First Intermediate Period at least, amulets were well spread out over a length of intricately twisted and knotted thread made from flax fibre. The tradition continued into the Roman Period, when some bodies wore over the chest a palm-fibre frame twisted around with flax thread to hold well-spaced-out amulets in rows. However, in the case of many Egyptian amulets, threading holes or suspension loops were not necessary since funerary examples intended purely for the tomb could be laid on the mummy or within its wrappings.

The first recognisable amulets occur as early as the predynastic Badarian Period, which predates the beginning of the First Dynasty in 3100 BC by more than a thousand years. All of them were found in burials, yet it is evident that their magical properties were primarily intended to provide aid in life; it was only subsequently that they were taken to the grave. Although very limited in form and material, these earliest amulets give a good indication of the dangerous forces which the early Egyptians felt were present in their world and needed to be harnessed by magical means. In some instances, too, they mark the first appearance of types which were to continue in use throughout dynastic history. Hobbled hippopotamus shapes, sometimes just the heads alone, suggest that, as in historic times, the river horse was considered a creature of unpredictable moods, most of them malevolent. An amulet in its form, especially an incapacitated one, was presumably intended to act apotropaically, rendering harmless this most dangerous animal by means of its own tethered representation and thereby affording protection to its wearer.

3b

Another equally early representational amulet appears to have the shape of an ante-

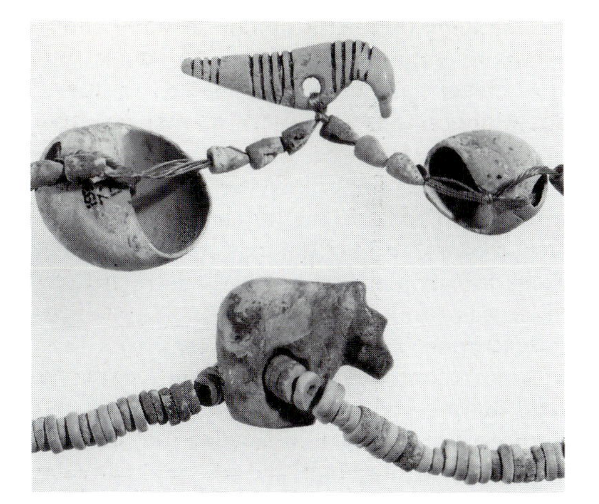

3 *Predynastic amulets.*
a) TOP Ivory archaic-form falcon with characteristic decoration strung with *Conus* and *Nerita* shells. Naqada 2; from Mostagedda. b) BOTTOM Shell tethered hippopotamus, one of the earliest Egyptian amulets known, strung with shell beads. H. 2 cm; Badarian; from el-Badari.

lope's or gazelle's head. In historic times, in one context at least, this creature was considered an embodiment of evil. Consequently an amulet in its shape might have been intended to avert ill-will or malevolence. However, at such an early date perhaps it was only hoped that by a kind of sympathetic magic its wearer might be given the animal's fleetness of foot or at least rendered a great hunter of this desert creature. Other early amulets in the shape of an animal's head, such as that of a panther or lioness, a dog and a bull, may also have incorporated the idea of protection by aversion. Yet they too might just as well have been felt capable of endowing their wearer with the ferocity of the big cat, the fleetness or slyness of the wild dog and the savage strength and virility of the bull. A definitive interpretation of an amulet's function in any period is often difficult; in the preliterate Predynastic Period only speculation is possible.

70f

Other recognisable amulets of predynastic date are the couchant jackal and the archaic-form crouched falcon, which in historic times would represent respectively the gods Anubis and Horus, both with protective capabilities. But how are early fly and hedgehog amulets to be interpreted? A final category of predynastic amulet is formed by natural objects such as birds' claws and shells of various types including the cowrie which, in particular, was to retain its amuletic significance until the end of pharaonic history. In dynastic times all such forms would come to be imitated in materials such as precious metal and semi-precious stones.

3a

By the end of this early period, stone pendants were a fairly common adornment. Usually they are little more than smoothed pebbles, presumably chosen for their colouring, but occasionally it is clear that they have been shaped and it is tempting to see a resemblance to amuletic forms. In one instance at least, long flat scutiform pendants may imitate a palette-shaped amulet with the knob at the top representing a stylised animal – or bird-head, just as in contemporary full-sized palettes on which eye-paint ingredients were ground down.

Surprisingly little has survived of amulets and amuletic jewellery from the Early Dynastic Period, but what there is shows a great advance in the quality of workmanship and the range of materials employed. In particular, to the early repertoire of glazed steatite and composition, ivory, shell and stones, some of them semi-precious, was added gold, perhaps the most characteristic of all Egyptian materials. A fine illustration of all these points is one of the four bracelets which miraculously survived on a wrapped arm found in the tomb of the First Dynasty pharaoh Djer at Abydos. It is composed of twenty-seven alternating gold and turquoise amuletic beads, each in the form of a *serekh*, a rectangular plaque decorated with characteristic palace façade panelling and surmounted by a falcon (in this case the crouched archaic type) which usually contained that element of the royal titulary termed the Horus name, thus associating the king with and placing him under the protection of the ancient falcon-form sky god. Of similar date are three hollow gold amulets found in a woman's burial at Nag ed-Deir. One comprises a foil elaterid beetle, its top surface incised and inlaid with the emblems of the goddess Neith, and would presumably have placed its owner under the goddess's protection. The second, an oryx with a Girdle Tie of the goddess Isis (*tit*) about its neck, and the third, a bull lacking horns and wearing a *Bat*-amulet, fetish of the goddess Hathor, were also probably protective.

66l

5c

Precious metal amuletic jewellery is also found, although rarely, in the succeeding Old Kingdom. A necklace discovered around the neck of a woman buried at Giza is composed of fifty hollow gold elaterid beetles, emblem of Neith, and again would have placed the owner under the goddess's protection. However, most contemporary amulets are of less precious materials, the most common being glazed composition, and are often so crudely formed as to be barely identifiable. Indeed, it is a curious fact that many early Egyptian amulets occur in what can only be called a debased form when they first appear.

Most of the new amuletic types which make their appearance during the later Old Kingdom represent animate objects. The frog, always connected with fertility, was probably worn by a woman, as must have been the amulet in the shape of the upright female hippopotamus, which would come to represent the goddess Thoeris, protectress of women in childbirth. (39) An amulet shaped like a duckling perhaps acted as a substitute food offering, but was this (4h) also the function of those in fish shape? Cows' heads with gracefully shaped horns represented the goddess Hathor, and the vulture was perhaps the manifestation of the goddess Nekhbet, patroness of Upper Egypt. A lion symbolised ferocity and regenerative powers; the double lion represented the region where the sun rose. (4c, 67c) But what was the function of an amuletic grasshopper or locust and a hare? (5g) An amulet shaped like a turtle, a creature of darkness, took the form of the very entity its wearer wished to avoid and thus acted apotropaically. (4a, 67g) Such was probably also the purpose of carefully shaped scorpions rather than that they were emblems of Serqet, even if she came to be a protective goddess. (4k) Crocodile amulets too were most likely used aversively rather than as animal manifestations of the god Sobk. (4d) For the first time amulets occur in the form of a human with an animal head: a jackal-headed deity is presumably Anubis. A kneeling man holding palm ribs can only be Heh, 'god of millions'. (4e)

The earliest amulet shaped like an *ankh* – today often erroneously called 'the key of life' – dates to the Old Kingdom. Now too the *wedjat*-eye makes its first appearance. (4i) Representing the left moon-eye of the falcon-form sky god Horus, it was one of the most powerful of all protective amulets. New also is the *djed*-pillar, though at first barely recognisable, one of the

4 *Early amuletic forms of Old Kingdom and First Intermediate Period date.* FROM LEFT TO RIGHT a) Olivine turtle. H. 1.3 cm. b) Olivine fly. c) Cornelian double lions' foreparts, joined. d) Ivory crocodile. e) Bone Heh, H. 1.8 cm. f) Pink limestone falcon. g) Ivory couchant dog or lion. h) Ivory duckling. i) Ivory *wedjat*-eye. j) Ivory *Tilapia*. k) Ivory scorpion. L. 2.4 cm. l) Ivory bee.

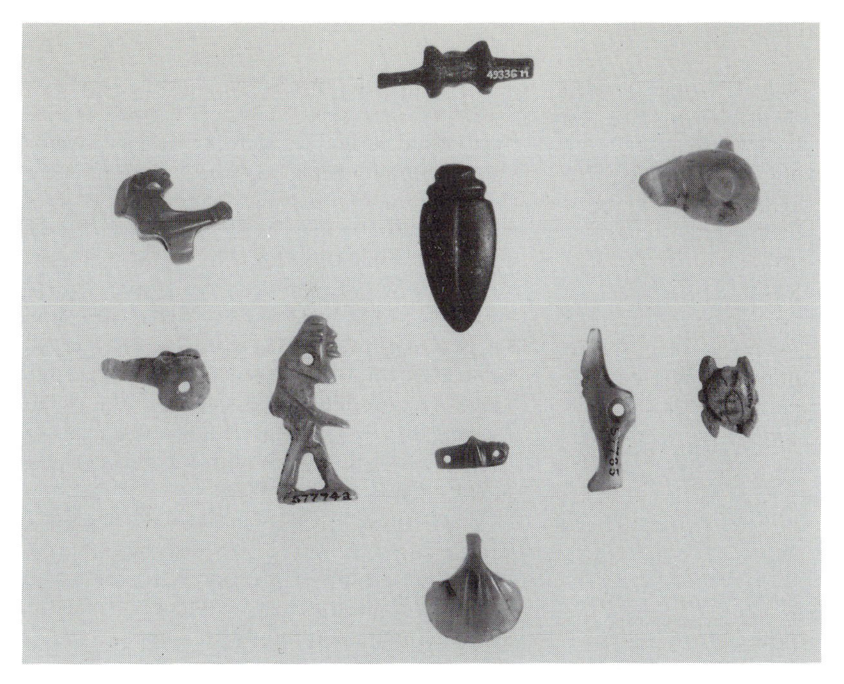

5 *Early amuletic forms.* From TOP, LEFT to RIGHT a) Min's emblem in wood: a door bolt or two fossil shells. OK, from Abydos. b) Cornelian lion's forepart. FIP. c) Black steatite beetle. FIP. d) Cornelian lioness' head in the round. FIP. e) Bone dog's head. OK. f) Bone 'kilted' man. H. 2.7 cm, OK. g) Cornelian stylised grasshopper or locust. OK to FIP. h) Cornelian 'hatted' man. FIP. i) Ivory scarab, one of the earliest known. OK, from Abydos. j) Cornelian *cardium edule* shell. OK.

most important prescribed funerary amulets which gave stability to the mummy's backbone. Just as early is the first appearance in an incredibly stylised form of the best known of all types of Egyptian amulet, that in the shape of the scarab or dung beetle. Considered symbolic of new life, regeneration and resurrection, it would come to be provided with even greater magical potency by the hieroglyphs and scenes added to its flat underside. 5i

Throughout this early period a considerable number of human-form amulets were produced, generally of very crude manufacture. Most appear to be male, a few female and fewer still children, the last so identified purely because they hold a finger to the mouth, the standard way of representing children during the Dynastic Period. However, further categorisation can only be arbitrary: some suggestions have included 'crouched', 'hatted', 'bearded', 'plain', 'walking' and 'kilted', though the last named can also be seen as ithyphallic, depending on the viewpoint. 5h 5f

But it was essentially during the succeeding First Intermediate Period that amulets buried with the dead (and sometimes worn by the living) increased greatly in numbers and expanded yet more their range of forms. Especially characteristic of the period are those shaped like parts of the body, which not only endowed their owners with their particular bodily functions, but could also even act as physical replacements should those parts be damaged. Now too amulets in the form of royal regalia appear, evidence of the democratisation of funerary beliefs which were once exclusively royal. 67d–f, 74 75, 62b–d

The Middle Kingdom saw a further increase in the repertoire of amuletic forms, although some, such as the precious-metal oyster-shell, cylinder amulet and knot clasp and the hardstone crouched proto-*Ba* or female sphinx, are virtually exclusive to the period. Particularly characteristic are amuletic cloisonné-work motto clasps from contemporary royal burials in which good-luck wishes or protective statements are spelled out in hieroglyphs made of inlaid gold. At this time the scarab also attained its fully recognisable form, often being worn on a cord purely as an amulet, its potency rendered even greater by an amuletic design carved on its underside. The greatest number of all, however, bore instead the title and name of their owners, sometimes too the name of the pharaoh they served; and, set for the first time as a finger-ring bezel, the scarab served as a seal. Until the introduction of the solid-metal signet ring in the Eighteenth Dynasty, the scarab was pre-eminent as a seal, at one and the same time functional because of its inscription and amuletic because of its shape. 43d 42, 49b 78b–c 45a, d

Before the New Kingdom amulets of deities,

6 *Multiple deities.*
a) Four figures with cat heads, two wearing feathers, standing with their backs against a square column. Turquoise-blue glazed composition. H. 4.2 cm TIP, possibly from Abydos.
b) Turquoise-blue glazed-composition finger-ring, the shank ending in a lily of Upper Egypt at one end and the papyrus of Lower Egypt at the other. The bezel is surmounted by two falcons each standing on a prostrate bound prisoner. Ramesside.
c) Four Bes figures in plumes, in pale green glazed composition, stand back to back to form a square. LP. d) Two standing falcons, each in tall plumes, representing two forms of Monthu. Pale green glazed composition. TIP.

whether human, animal-headed or in sacred animal form, are conspicuously few and at first the repertoire is narrow. The minor deities Thoeris, goddess of childbirth, her leonine helper Bes and dwarfish *pataikos* are most popular. Only a few of the major deities such as the falcon-form sun god, Isis suckling Horus and Hathor as cow are found. However, from the end of the New Kingdom until the end of dynastic history, such figures are the most numerous and diverse in range. All the great gods and goddesses, as well as some of their less well-known divine colleagues, appear as amulets. Thus among lion-headed figures are found not only Sekhmet, Bastet and Wadjyt but Pakhet and Mehyt and the fierce god Mayhes. Certain deities are characteristic of a particular period. Groups of the Four Sons of Horus, protectors of the mummified internal organs, do not appear before the Third Intermediate Period because of a change in embalming practices. It was in the same period that cat-form amulets representing the goddess Bastet and elaborate amuletic counterpoises surmounted by an *aegis* were most popular.

39 37c 30, 19a, c 23b 50, 51 29 40

Plaques with a high raised relief triad of Isis, Nephthys and Horus-the-Child do not occur before the Saite Period. This was also the time when funerary amulets increased significantly in number. In some instances this was because forms such as the headrest amulet, which before had been placed only in royal burials were now available to the non-royal dead. In addition, in line with the archaising trends of the period, some types of amulet which had not been used for fifteen centuries were revived. One such example was the double-lion amulet. Moreover, new forms were invented, like the two-fingers amulet, which it was felt perhaps ought to have existed earlier.

back cover 95 91a 73e, 6

When W.M.F. Petrie published his seminal work *Amulets* in 1914, he divided the 275 types known to him into five great classes for which he coined the terms homopoeic, dynatic, ktematic, phylactic and theophoric.

By homopoeic Petrie meant amulets of similars: that is, those in the form of a living creature or part of a living creature which by assimilation would endow its wearer with the creature's characteristic powers or capabilities. His dynatic category is closely connected, except in this class the amulets are in the shape of generally inanimate objects invested with particular powers whose use could be transferred to their wearers. Petrie termed ktematic (from the Greek word for property) amulets which represented on the one hand the possessions of the living, such as clothing and personal accoutrements which were taken to the tomb for use in the Afterlife, and on the other hand funerary goods such as equipment for the mummy or food offerings which were connected purely with the burial and funerary cult. Should the actual objects be stolen, destroyed or, in the case of the food offerings, not presented, the amuletic representations of them would magically act as substitutes. If proof were needed of the difficulties inherent in attempting to classify amulets into even as few as five broad categories, it can be provided easily here. Amulets in the shape of human bodily parts could substitute for those members or organs should the mummy be damaged. However, the chief function of such amulets is, of course, to be found under the heading of homopoeic.

The fourth class of phylactic (protective)

amulets comprises those which can be animate or inanimate in form. But it is Petrie's final category of theophoric (or, better still, theomorphic) amulets – that is, those in the shape of deities or their animal manifestations – which is the most contentious although the easiest to identify. Most theomorphic amulets would be worn to place their wearer under the protection or patronage of the deity depicted and are thus phylactic. The remainder are surely homopoeic in function since their wearer would hope to assimilate the person of the deity represented and thus gain access to the deity's particular powers or characteristics.

In addition to these difficulties Petrie's work was published before most of the site excavation reports which were to be the sources for a great number of well-dated and closely identified examples of amulets. Those of Matmar, Mostagedda, Qaw and Badari have proved indispensible. Of course, Tutankhamun's treasures and the royal burials at Tanis were unknown to him. Yet Petrie's general system of classification remains usable and so the layout of this publication follows it, if only in broad outline. His illustrations of the positions of amulets on twenty-four Late Period mummies also remain of great value. It must always be remembered, moreover, that although virtually every Egyptian collection, whatever its size, can claim to contain amulets, often in considerable numbers, until very recently only a handful of 'star' or typical examples were published. It is only now that attempts are being made to produce and publish in a systematic manner comprehensive catalogues of small antiquities, including every amulet however unlovely or damaged. Only in this way can comparative studies be carried out to reveal whether known amulets are correctly dated or even representative in form or material. On this basis, of course, the present publication cannot pretend to be comprehensive. Its main source is the amuletic collection in the Department of Egyptian Antiquities of the British Museum used in conjunction with W. M. F. Petrie, *Amulets* (London, 1914), G. A. Reisner, *Amulets (CG)*, I/II (Cairo, 1907/1958), C. Müller-Winkler, *Die Ägyptischen Objekt-Amulette* (Freiburg, 1987) and B. Schlick-Nolte and V. V. Droste zu Hülshoff, *Liebieghaus-Frankfort am Main, Ägyptische Bildwerke I, Skarabäen, Amulette und Schmuck* (Melsungen, 1990).

7 *Degenerate forms of amulets.* From LEFT to RIGHT a) Grey-green glazed-composition kneeling Shu with upraised arms. LP. b) Pale turquoise-blue glazed-composition *ankh*. LP. c) Pale green glazed- composition double *wedjat*-eye. LP. d) Pale turquoise-blue glazed-composition *wedjat*-eye. W. 1.1 cm, LP. e) Grey-green glazed-composition walking ibis-headed Thoth. LP. f) Grey-green glazed-composition walking Anubis. LP. g) Bright turquoise- blue glazed-composition ape- headed Hapy, flat backed with stitching holes. H. 6.1 cm, 25th Dynasty or later. h) Dark blue glass *tit*. G-R. i) Bright blue glass *djed*. Ptolemaic.

2

Amulets of Gods, Goddesses and Sacred Animals

The large number of amulets in the shape of deities, whether completely human, with animal head or in sacred animal manifestation, comprises the category which Petrie termed theophoric but which is preferably called theomorphic from the Greek meaning 'in divine form'. However, in spite of the popular conception that there were 1,001 gods in the Egyptian pantheon, amulets were made in the likeness of only a small proportion of them. Of these some are instantly recognisable, others (best of all) are inscribed with the name of the deity in question, but a disappointing number, usually animal-headed, are difficult to identify. The problem is that the Egyptians believed most of their gods were able to manifest themselves in animal form, but there were so many deities that there were not enough types of animal to suffice. Thus any one species might represent a number of different gods. Monthu, Khonsu, Qebhsenuef and Sokaris, the different forms of the sun god, the three chief Horuses and their variants might all be represented by an amulet of a man with a falcon's head. Sekhmet, Tefnut, Mehyt, Pakhet and Bastet, even Wadjyt, might all appear as an amulet of a lion-headed woman.

51b, 50c, 13a, e, 26, 8c

19a, 30, 8a, b

Most of these figurines were made from green- or blue-glazed composition with some glass and semi-precious stones; less common are metal examples, both bronze and precious. In the case of bronze figurines it is sometimes difficult to be certain whether the object should be classified as an amulet. In the Late Period it was the practice to place a mummified sacred animal (if tiny enough), or part of it, in a bronze reliquary surmounted by a bronze representation of the creature in question. A number of these reliquaries are not only small and light enough to have been worn as a pendant amulet, but they actually have suspension loops. On the other hand, some with loops are far too bulky and heavy to have been worn. Similarly, some metal figurines of deities, although small enough, have suspension loops so placed (for example, only behind the ankles) that they would have been impossible to wear in a sensible fashion. All such figures and reliquaries must rather have been set up as a focus for veneration. Two-dimensional images of de-

8 *Tiny, superbly shaped figures of deities.*
a) Deep Egyptian-blue lion-headed walking goddess, wearing a uraeus and holding a papyrus sceptre. The back-pillar names Bastet. H. 4.3 cm, late TIP to Saite. b) Seated lion-headed goddess in red jasper. LD. c) Squatting falcon-headed figure, perhaps the funerary god Sokaris. Lapis lazuli. LD.

9 *Miniature shrines.*
a) Bronze shrine decorated with seated deities (Maat, Khnum, Khonsu, Thoth and Re-Horakhty). Its inscription names king Tuthmosis III. The underside, inscribed 'the estate of Amun', can function as a stamp-seal. The bronze solid-cast seated figure of Amen-Re was inside the shrine. H. of shrine 10.7 cm, 18th Dynasty, *c.* 1450 BC. b) Openwork green glazed steatite shrine with two-leafed door, decorated at the back with a winged scarab and at the sides with a seated solar lion-headed goddess. The smaller shrine within contains an *aegis* of a solar lion-headed goddess. H. 4.8 cm, TIP.

ities were also shaped from glazed composition and glass, (often polychrome), in an open-backed mould or were merely incised on a plaque.

Many theomorphic amulets would have been worn purely to place their wearer, whether dead or alive, under the protection of a particular deity; these are dealt with in Chapter 3. The remainder are either homopoeic in function, since the wearer would hope to assimilate the person of the deity represented and thus gain access to their particular powers or characteristics, or they were worn to show patronage by or devotion to the deity. Thus a man born in Gebelein might choose to wear an amulet in the form of the local god Sobk, or a priest of Khnum one of the ram-headed deity. Obviously the dividing line is extremely tenuous. This category is subdivided into human gods and goddesses and animal-headed or animal-form deities.

Male Human-Form Deities

Most completely **human** deities were very ancient, often originally worshipped as an inanimate object such as a fossil or tree, like Min or Nut. When the Egyptians anthropomorphised their gods, it was these primordial deities who were distinguished by not being animal-headed, although they did usually have an animal form in which they could appear. **Amen-Re**, however, the Theban god of empire, although usually depicted completely human, was not one of these very ancient deities. Originally, as **Amun**, he was the male element of one of the four couples worshipped at Hermopolis (Ashmunein) – his female consort was Amunet – who by the Middle Kingdom had established himself at Thebes. When the local princes reunited Egypt, Amun became important. When Theban princes drove out the Hyksos and founded the Eighteenth Dynasty nearly five hundred years later, Amun became pre-eminent; united with the sun god to give him universal appeal, Amen-Re became king of the gods.

A visual clue to Amen-Re's false antiquity,

however, is that as an amulet, wearing long beard and short kilt, he walks; primordial male deities like Min or Ptah have bound legs. His characteristic headgear is a low round crown surmounted by the sun-disc of Re and two tall feathers, perhaps a pictorial reference to his name: *Imn* means 'hidden' and hence 'the wind', and only ruffled feathers could indicate his unseen presence. Amulets of Amen-Re, sometimes depicting him in profile squatting, 38c but always with characteristic low crown and feathers, do not predate the Third Intermediate Period. Moreover, apart from being very rare they are usually of precious metal or very well-modelled glazed composition, which suggests that they were worn in life to show his patronage of those in his service. For his animal manifestation see **rams** (page 30).

For **Heh** *see page 89.*

Some New Kingdom burials contained flat-backed amulets in cornelian, red jasper and 10c, d glass depicting a kilted squatting figure in profile with finger to the lips and wearing 64a the broad-tressed side-lock of the period. In identically postured glazed-composition examples found at el Amarna the figure wears a crown. This suggests a link on the one hand with amulets like the solid-gold squatting pendant of Tutankhamun crowned and carrying a crook and flail, and on the other with a Ramesside inlaid gold pendant of a figure with side-lock squatting on a lotus, both symbolic of the newly born or **infant sun**. By the Third Intermediate Period, however, the only comparable amulets, made in the round from glazed composition or bronze, portray a naked figure wearing a side-lock with triple *atef*-crown or 10e, f *nemes* wig-cover or else wearing only a side-lock, sometimes with finger to the mouth, sometimes carrying a crook, either squatting or 101b in the curious half-standing, half-sitting posture unique to **Horus-the-Child** (in Greek, 10 Harpocrates). Henceforth, throughout the Late Period, all amulets of this type represent only Horus-the-Child, the infant son of Isis and Osiris, for whose protection his mother wove potent spells which would be accessible to the amulet's wearer (see also page 49).

As architect of the Step Pyramid of the Third Dynasty pharaoh Djoser at Saqqara, **Imhotep** was soon revered as a wise man, but 11a

10 *Horus-the-Child.* From LEFT to RIGHT a) Horus-the-Child made in black steatite, wearing a side lock and standing on a crocodile. Its tail is held in the right hand. LP. b) In pale turquoise-blue glazed composition, wearing a side lock and standing with finger to the lips. H. 7.4 cm, TIP. c) Flat-backed, in red glazed composition, squatting with finger to the lips. He wears a kilt and Amarna-style side tress. H. 2.8 cm, 18th Dynasty. d) In blue-green glazed composition, flat-backed and squatting with finger to the lips, wearing a side lock. NK. e) Pale green glazed composition, squatting, wearing *nemes* with a side lock and holding a crook. Saite. f) Horus-the-Child squatting and wearing a triple *atef*-crown with side lock, in turquoise-blue glazed composition. TIP.

11 *Human-form deities.*
a) Imhotep, seated with a papyrus roll open on the lap. Pale turquoise-blue glazed composition. Saite. b) Bronze solid-cast ithyphallic Min in double plumes, with a flail over the right hand. TIP. c) Pale green glazed-composition Ptah, wrapped like a mummy, wearing a skull cap and archaic beard and carrying a combined *djed* and *was*. H. 6.9 cm, LD. d) Pale green glazed-composition Khonsu wrapped like a mummy, carrying symbols of power and wearing the full and crescent moon, uraeus and side-lock. H. 3.7 cm, Saite. e) Grey-green glazed-composition kneeling Shu supporting a sun disc. Saite.

by the Saite Period he had been deified (and was considered the son of Ptah), one of only a handful of historical non-royal Egyptians to enjoy such an honour. In the Twenty-sixth Dynasty and later, amulets were made in glazed composition, lapis lazuli and bronze depicting him seated in long kilt and skull-cap with a papyrus open on his lap, exactly as he was represented in large votive bronzes of the period. Since Imhotep was also connected with healing, an amulet in his form might have been worn to give some kind of medical aid or protection.

, 38d

Small bronze and silver amulets in the round of **Inhert** (Greek Onuris), an ancient warrior god of the Abydos area, occasionally occur in Late Period burials. Characteristically, he wears a long kilt, a beard and a short wig surmounted by two tall plumes and his right arm is raised above his shoulder to hurl a lance which is rarely depicted; his left hand holds to his stomach a dangling cord. His name, which means 'Returner of the Distant One', refers to how he brought back the wandering lioness-form Eye of the Sun.

11d

Only small Late Period glazed-composition amulets in the round, one firmly dated to the Twenty-sixth Dynasty, represent **Khonsu** in human form. Khonsu was the Theban moon god who was considered the child of Amen-Re and Mut. He appears as a mummiform figure with only his hands emerging to grasp various emblems of power; he wears a beard, uraeus and side-lock and a moon with crescent on his head. A variant adult version usually identified as **Iah**, which means 'moon', occurs as a bronze amulet depicting a standing bearded man carrying a tall staff, who wears a long tripartite wig and a moon with crescent surmounted by an *atef*-crown with a further disc above it. Late Period plaques depicting Khonsu with his divine parents show a falcon-headed man. See also **falcon-form** deities (page 30).

12a

11b

Of all the Egyptian gods represented in completely human form the one most instantly recognisable is **Min** or **Amen-ka-mutef**. As god of virility and procreative powers he is always depicted as ithyphallic, wrapped like a mummy with one hand raising a flail over his right shoulder and wearing two tall feathers on a low round crown. Amulets in this form occur unusually early: one in gold was found in a Twelfth Dynasty burial at Abydos. However, they are a particular feature of the Late Period, made of bronze or glazed composition in the round and presumably worn by men in order to assimilate the god's virile powers.

12 *Solid-cast metal anthropoid gods.*
a) Bronze moon-god Iah wearing full and crescent moons from which emerges an ibis head, all surmounted by an *atef*-crown. LP. b) Bronze Inhert in a long kilt, short wig and four plumes in a square, with upraised arm and a rope or weapon held close to his body. LP. c) Silver Nefertum with an open lotus and plumes on his head. H. 12.6 cm, TIP. d) Silver Osiris carrying a crook and flail, wearing the *atef*-crown. TIP to LP.

13 *Groups of deities.*
a) Ivory modelled three-dimensional falcon-headed Horus standing beside his father Osiris, on a plinth with back-pillar. TIP or later. b) Pale green glazed-composition modelled triad of Memphis: lion-headed Sekhmet wearing disc, Ptah on a stepped dais and Nefertum. The back of the supporting plaque asks for life from the three deities. H. 2.2 cm, Saite. c) Bronze solid-cast jackal-headed walking Anubis, holding upright before him his father, Osiris. LP. d) Green-blue glazed-composition Nefertum wearing characteristic lotus and plumes seated beside his mother, lion-headed Sekhmet who wears a uraeus. The back-pillar has good luck emblems. LD. e) Bright turquoise-blue glazed-composition plaque with three high modelled relief figures of the Theban triad: falcon-headed Khonsu, Amen-Re and Mut in Double Crown, holding hands. The back names Amen-Re, Lord of the Two Lands, Ruler of the Gods. H. 4.6 cm, LD.

Nefertum, who wears on his head a lotus surmounted by two tall plumes, came to be linked with Ptah and Sekhmet to form the divine family of the Memphite area. In the Twenty-sixth Dynasty small glazed-composition plaques have the three in high relief on one side and their names, totally unnecessarily, on the other. But his origins were ancient: in one creation legend it was a sweet-smelling blue lotus which first appeared on the waters of primordial chaos. Only when its petals opened was the sun god revealed. Amulets of Nefertum in a short kilt in the round, both walking and seated, made from glazed composition, bronze, silver and later glass, first occur in the early Third Intermediate Period. An unusual Late Dynastic type in well-modelled glazed composition depicts the god standing on the

12c

13b, d

back of a couchant or walking lion, his animal manifestation. Sometimes a couchant lion on its own wears the god's distinctive headgear. 21d

For **Osiris** *see page 47.*

Amulets of **Ptah**, the ancient creator god of Memphis, patron of craftsmen, depict a distinctive mummiform figure, wearing a skull-cap and straight beard, with only his hands emerging to grasp a *was*-sceptre or multiple sceptre to his body. They are, however, surprisingly rare. Apart from a few in bronze and glazed composition and a couple in cast gold and foil over a core, all of Late Dynastic date, the finest and earliest example comes from the Twenty-first Dynasty burial of Wendjebauendjed at Tanis. The lapis lazuli figure holding a *djed*-pillar – as much his emblem as that of Osiris – had lost its feet in antiquity, but was still considered important enough to set within a superbly decorated gold shrine with a suspension loop on the roof so that the piece could be worn like a reliquary. His unusual head-dress of disc and feathers suggests the composite primordial creator god **Ptah-Tatenen**. He stands flanked by a double pair of free-standing gold solar falcons on papyrus columns and the outer walls of the shrine are a mass of relief squatting deities in pairs, six per side, two per row, no doubt representing his fellow temple gods. c, 38g, 16e, 98d

Plaque-form amulets of the Memphite triad of Ptah, Sekhmet and Nefertum, made in glazed composition, are Twenty-sixth Dynasty in date. (For Ptah's animal manifestation see **Apis Bull**, page 24). 13b

In the Heliopolitan version of creation, **Shu** was the son of the sun, the principle of air, who, with his consort Tefnut, the principle of moisture, created Geb and Nut, earth and sky, whom he promptly separated by raising Nut aloft. In amuletic form this explanation of how the air comes to support heaven, the sun's domain, is symbolised by Shu in a short kilt kneeling on his right knee with his arms raised aloft in the attitude of the *ka* with the sun-disc between. For technical reasons the sun is directly on top of his head and the spaces between the arms and his head are in-filled. Although some very crude glazed-composition amulets of this type are already found in Third Intermediate Period burials, finely modelled examples in the round date to the Twenty- 11e, 7a

14 *Unusual anthropomorphic deities.*
a) Green-blue glazed-composition seated Shu in a long garment, short wig and tall plumes, clasps a *was*-sceptre under his chin. The throne sides have a solar falcon with raised wings. H. 6.2 cm, TIP. b) A unique wooden amulet of a king, in Double Crown, tripartite wig and beard, treading on two negro heads, symbolising royal power. NK to TIP. c) Blue-green glazed-composition Mut (named on back-pillar), in a Double Crown with uraeus and wearing horns and disc, incongruously suckles an infant god as she walks. TIP.

sixth Dynasty and were placed on the lower torso of mummies. Sometimes the sun-disc is not depicted, but the posture remains the same. Sometimes a feather symbolising 'air' and the god's name is cursorily represented within the disc. Otherwise the usual representation of Shu with a feather or feathers on his head is found in an amuletic context only surmounting the *aegis* of counterpoises beside the head of Tefnut. One rare glazed-composition amulet, however, depicts him sitting in a long kilt resting his beardless chin on a *was*-sceptre and wearing a short wig surmounted by double feathers. Rather unusual glazed-composition amulets of Third Intermediate Period date depicting a man in tall plumes and long kilt seated next to a lion-headed woman probably represent Shu with his consort Tefnut, but it is just possible that Inhert and Mehyt are intended. 40d, 14a

Female Human-Form Deities

One of the most ancient and greatest of goddesses was **Hathor**: gauge her antiquity from her name, which means 'Mansion of Horus', the earliest god. When mentioned in the Old

Kingdom *Pyramid Texts*, she was already patroness of Sinai, Byblos and Punt (Somalia). She was celestial mother of the sun calf, protectress of the necropolis, goddess of love and music, nurse of pharaoh and consort of Horus of Edfu, and her cult centres lay all along the Nile valley, but especially at Dendera. Her 15c, e, 31d characteristic guise was a woman with heavy plaits and cow's ears, a memory of her bovine form, but just as often she wears horns and a disc which can lead to confusion with Isis, especially as the two became virtually one entity in the Late Period. Often only an inscription can allow certain identification. However, the head surmounting an *aegis* amulet is certainly Hathor's because of her link with the *menyet* collar.

Whether or not *boukrania* amulets (see page 62) originally represented Hathor or Bat, the goddess of the Seventh Upper Egyptian nome, by the Middle Kingdom the former had completely subsumed the latter and all her attributes. From the Eighteenth Dynasty, Hathor-head amulets always depict the goddess with heavy plaits and cow's ears and, made from hollow and cast gold, semi-precious stones, glazed composition and glass, they were produced until the end of dynastic history. Even the Meroitic Queen Amanishakheto owned a necklace formed from eleven hollow gold Hathor-heads inlaid with blue glass. During the New Kingdom the backs of scaraboids were sometimes carved into the shape of Hathor-heads.

An amuletic figure of a walking or seated woman in the round with or without a papyrus sceptre and wearing cow's horns and a disc 18a, 17b might be Hathor or Isis. Such figures first appear in precious metal in the early Third Intermediate Period: a tiny finely detailed solid-gold seated example was found in the Twenty-Second Dynasty burial of Prince Hornakht at Tanis and an unprovenanced walking one is probably of a similar date. However, a particularly splendid solid-gold standing example on a gold chain from Wendjebauendjed's burial at Tanis is specifically named as Isis. Both seated and standing forms occur just as early in glazed composition and, by the Late Period, in bronze and in mould-made and modelled glass too. 16d Probably only female figures with a cow's head are indisputably Hathor. Of two datable examples, both representing the goddess standing and carrying a papyrus sceptre, one, wearing double plumes and incised into sheet gold, came from a Saite burial; the other, of cast gold, originated from a burial of Thirtieth Dynasty date. Other hollow-gold unprovenanced pieces must be of the same late period. The material may be a punning reference to Hathor's epithet of 'the golden one', although glazed-composition examples are also known.

15 *Divine heads and busts.*
a) Sheet gold repoussé Bes head pierced for attachment. LP. b) Fourteen hollow sheet-gold ancestor busts and one hollow sheet-gold fly amulet strung with two cornelian beads. Life-sized stone ancestor busts were the household gods of an Egyptian home. 18th Dynasty. c) Bone flat-backed Hathor head with cow's ears. MK. d) Dark green glazed-composition flat-backed Bes head. H. 3.1 cm, TIP. e) Turquoise-blue glazed-composition double-faced Hathor head with heavy plaits and cow's ears. TIP or later.

A rare glazed-composition amulet of Hathor with cow's head, horns, disc and plumes depicts her suckling a child god seated on her lap, but as mother of the sky calf and representative of all the most admired maternal qualities she most often assumed the guise of a complete cow, usually with a disc between her horns; a 21b cow amulet is depicted in the MacGregor 16b Papyrus list. However, not only are bovine amulets, especially when kneeling, notoriously difficult to sex, but other goddesses such as Nut, Isis and Mehweret the primordial flood took the same form. A kneeling cow amulet in sheet gold first occurs in a Twenty-sixth Dynasty burial; flat-backed glass examples are 66c typically Ptolemaic. The few bronze cow amulets in the round are probably Late Dynastic in date. Far commoner, though, are rectangular plaques bearing a representation of a walking cow, often with a lotus at her neck: the Eighteenth Dynasty burial of the wives of Tuthmosis III contained three of embossed gold; examples in glass and bronze with incised cows and holes for suspension are characteristic of the Late Dynastic period.

Uniquely, the goddess of the nome of Mendes in the delta is represented in amuletic form as a woman wearing over the top and down the back of her bewigged head a creature which has been formerly identified incorrectly as a dolphin but is actually a *Schilbe*, the sacred fish of the area. It is characterised by its humped posture, which actually helps to form the suspension loop. Most appropriately the goddess is called **Hatmehyt**, 'Foremost of the Fishes', (17c) and glazed-composition examples of her in the round, both seated and standing, are first found in Third Intermediate Period burials. *Schilbe*-shaped amuletic beads in various materials, worn as emblems of the goddess, are (93a, f) also known.

For **Isis** *see page 48.*

Maat represents all kinds of abstract concepts, such as cosmic order, truth, justice and righteousness, personified as a squatting woman, her hands on her knees and single ostrich plume on her head. Although the burial of the wives of Tuthmosis III contained a string of flat gold plaques incised with the goddess's figure and a single plaque with the goddess

16 ABOVE *Gold funerary amulets.*
a) Sheet-metal Heh kneeling and holding palm ribs. LD. b) Foil plaque incised with amulets and amuletic jewellery, exactly like those depicted in the MacGregor papyrus amulets list: vultures, *afnet* wig, heart, collar with falcon-headed terminals, mace, sceptre, serpent, crook and flail, counterpoises, *wadj*, *wedjat*, *djed*, *tit*, *sweret*, cow, sistrum, uraeus and *was*. W. 4.6 cm; LP. c) Human-headed canopic deity Imsety leans against the emblem of the West. Openwork sheet metal. LP. d) Hollow sheet-metal Hathor with a cow's head wearing disc and plumes. LD. e) Hollow sheet-metal (but flattened) Ptah holding a *was* sceptre with his name written before his face. H. 4.2 cm, LP.

17 LEFT *Uncommon female deities.*
a) Bright turquoise-blue glazed-composition Satet or Nekhbet as a woman wearing the White Crown flanked by feathers. There is a cobra-headed scorpion in place of a uraeus. TIP. b) Blue-green glazed-composition Isis in horns and disc, carrying a papyrus sceptre, protected by the winged arms of an identical figure at her back. H. 9.2 cm, late TIP. c) Grass-green glazed-composition seated Hatmehyt (named on the back-pillar) wearing the *Schilbe*, sacred fish of Mendes, on her head. TIP.

embossed on it, one of the earliest dated amulets of Maat in the round comes from the Twenty-second Dynasty burial of Hornakht at Tanis. Carved in profile from lapis lazuli, it is backed with moulded sheet gold and hangs from a gold strip ribbon. Other unprovenanced lapis lazuli examples in the round and silver ones too may be of similar date, although Late Period lapis pieces are known. A gold-foil Maat over a shaped core wearing an inlaid feather, still hanging from a magnificent gold loop-in-loop chain, might once have been worn as a Saite judge's insignia, as the Greek historian Herodotus records. Contemporary examples in the round in Egyptian blue (see p. 102) often lack the feather for manufacturing reasons. In the Ptolemaic Period the goddess's image was often fashioned from glass made in an open-backed mould. When found on the mummy, Maat amulets are on the chest.

The consort of Amen-Re at Thebes was **Mut**, a local vulture-form fertility and mother goddess. As an amulet she is depicted completely human, walking or sitting and wearing the Double Crown in her role of wife to the king of the gods. However, rather confusingly, she is also sometimes shown just like Isis suckling a male child (presumably Khonsu) who sits on her lap and is propped up by her left hand. All three types occur early in the Third Intermediate Period, often made of quite finely modelled glazed composition in the round, and all bear inscriptions naming the goddess as Mut, Lady of Isheru, her precinct at Karnak. A well-made solid-gold walking example is probably of similar date. In the same period Mut's head surmounts *aegis* and counterpoise amulets whose shape can also be

18 *Suckling goddesses.*
a) Blue-green glazed-composition Isis-Hathor, wearing a cow's horns and disc, suckles the infant Horus. There are winged goddesses on the sides of the throne. TIP. b) Bright-blue glazed-composition Isis, with the hieroglyph for her name on her head, suckling the infant Horus. H. 11.4 cm, Saite.
c) Grass-green glazed-composition Mut (named on the back pillar) wearing the Double Crown, her wig adorned with cobras, suckling an infant deity. H. 6.2 cm, TIP.

45e found as an element of contemporary openwork glazed-composition finger-rings. Sometimes, too, openwork and gold ring bezels de- 45i pict the goddess seated in majesty. Mut remained very popular in the Meroitic Period: a number of Queen Amanishakheto's inlaid gold shield rings and hinged armlets depict her as a central motif. Some Third Intermediate Period glazed-composition amulets of a woman 19c with a lion's head in a Double Crown and carrying a papyrus sceptre represent a syncretistic form of Mut and Sekhmet.

In the First Dynasty queens' names already incorporated that of the ancient warrior goddess **Neith**. Because of her antiquity she may have been depicted originally as an inanimate 82a, c fetish which later occurs as an amulet in its own right (see page 81) and which, as one of the four great protectresses of the dead, she usually wears on her head as her name. In amuletic form, however, Neith is depicted as a woman wearing the crown of Lower Egypt. A sheet-gold example of her squatting in profile comes from a Twenty-sixth Dynasty burial; lapis 20f lazuli and glazed-composition walking figures are of similar date. They are always placed on the mummy's chest. Neith's chief cult centre was at Sais in the delta, but at Esna she was venerated not only as the mother of all the gods but also of Sobk in particular, which is why in some Saite glazed-composition amuletic representations she suckles two large crocodiles, one 19b at each breast, their bodies clinging to hers. A gold-foil capsule in the shape of the **elaterid beetle**, sacred to Neith, inlaid with her emblems, was found in a First Dynasty burial at Nag ed-Deir; fifty sheet-gold examples beaten into a mould formed a Fourth Dynasty woman's necklace. Examples in glazed composition were still being placed in First Inter- 5c mediate Period burials. The Greeks called Esna 'Latopolis' after the *Lates* sacred to Neith; amulets in the shape of this fish, there- 93e fore, which occur in various materials from the late Old Kingdom onwards, might have been worn as emblems of the goddess.

For **Nephthys** *see page 48.*

A superbly modelled glazed-composition amulet of a walking woman wearing the White Crown flanked by feathers may be a rare representation of **Satet**, goddess of the first cata- 17a ract and consort of Khnum or possibly depicts

19 *Unusual forms of suckling goddesses.*
a) Grass-green glazed-composition standing lion-headed goddess, protected by the wings of a human goddess at her back, cups her breast to a standing child-god too small to reach. TIP. b) Pale green glazed-composition Neith in the Red Crown walks as she suckles a crocodile at each breast, symbolising her son Sobk. H. 8.6 cm, Saite. c) Flat-backed lion-headed goddess (Sekhmet-Mut), in the Double Crown, stands to suckle a pharaoh carrying the crook. Pale turquoise-blue glazed composition. TIP.

20 *Finely-formed small funerary amulets.*
a) Grey-green glazed-composition walking ibis-headed Thoth. Saite. b) Walking jackal-headed Anubis in pale turquoise-blue glazed composition. Saite. c) Walking falcon-headed Khonsu, wearing full and crescent moons. Pale turquoise-blue glazed composition. H 4.5 cm. Saite. d) Walking ram-headed Khnum in pale turquoise-blue glazed composition. Saite. e) Lapis lazuli walking Serqet wearing a scorpion on her head. LD. f) Lapis lazuli walking Neith wearing the Red Crown. LD. g) Pale turquoise-blue glazed-composition human-headed *Ba* bird. Saite.

Nekhbet, patroness of Upper Egypt. Because by the Late Period either might be associated, in her role of protectress, with the scorpion goddess Serqet (Greek Selkis), what appears at a cursory glance to be a uraeus on her crown is actually a detailed scorpion with a cobra's head.

Serqet herself was one of the four protectresses of the dead; her harmful powers were thus harnessed to be used for good. Although 4k scorpion-form amulets were made throughout the dynastic period from as early as the Old Kingdom, they could of themselves have been used apotropaically without being symbolic of the goddess. Serqet first appears in amuletic form as a walking woman with a scorpion on her bewigged head, and made in the round from glazed composition, in the Third Intermediate Period. Finely carved lapis lazuli 20e examples have been found on the upper chest of mummies of Thirtieth Dynasty date. Well-modelled bronze and glazed-composition scorpion amulets of late dynastic date with a female head wearing horns and disc represent Serqet with the attributes of Isis, probably with reference to the spells found on contemporary *cippi*.

Amulets in the form of **suckling goddesses** can represent **Hededet**, **Isis**, **Mut** or **Nehemtawy** (consort of Nehebkau). The only clue to their identity is that they wear on their heads respectively scorpions, cow's horns and disc, Double Crown, and sistrum.

Male Animal-headed and Animal Deities

For **Anubis** *see page 46.*

The history of the **Apis bull**, the animal manifestation of Ptah of Memphis, can be traced back to the beginning of the dynastic period. There was only one Apis at a time, chosen by his markings; once selected after his predecessor's death, he was installed near the temple of Ptah where he spent a life of luxury adored by pious worshippers, delivering oracles and entertained by his own harim of cows. When he died, the Apis was embalmed and entombed with all the solemnity and pomp of pharaoh himself in a huge granite sarcophagus inside a vault within the network of underground catacombs at Saqqara called the Serapeum. Votive bronzes of the Apis, with his distinctive markings, are characteristic of the Late Period, but amulets in his shape are rare. They would have been worn in life as a sign of special devotion; however, the god's later funerary significance in association with Osiris gave them a particular potency in the Other Life too. The Apis is represented as a walking 21a bull, sometimes wearing a sun-disc between his horns. He is made from bronze or glazed

21 *Sacred animals.*
a) Turquoise-blue glazed-composition walking Apis bull. L. 2.9 cm, Saite. b) Bronze walking cow, probably of Hathor, wearing disc and plumes between lyre-shaped horns. LP. c) Bronze jackal or wolf, most probably Wepwawet, on a sled flanked by two uraei. The inscription on the underside names only Osiris. TIP. d) Pale green glazed-composition couchant lion wearing the lotus and plumes of Nefertum. Saite. e) Turquoise-blue glazed-composition walking ram sacred to more than one deity. TIP. f) Turquoise-blue and dark blue glazed-composition squatting ibis of Thoth, the beak supported by the feather of Maat. L. 4.5 cm, LP.

composition in the round or from flat-backed moulded glass. There is rarely the possibility to delineate his particular markings, so there is always the chance that the **Buchis bull** sacred to Monthu or the **Mnevis bull** sacred to Re is intended. Extremely rarely the Apis is depicted as a bull-headed walking man. No amulets are earlier than the Late Period, when his worship was at its peak. The unique repoussé sheet-gold walking-bull amulet from a First Dynasty burial wears the fetish of Hathor around its neck, making identification with the Apis improbable.

For **Bes** *see page 39.*

23b **Mayhes** (Greek Miyses) is unique among lion-headed deities for, of all the amulets with a maned big cat's head, his alone represents a god not a goddess, always depicted as a walking man in a short kilt and wearing an *atef*-crown. Mayhes means 'savage lion' and appropriately he aided the sun god in the fight against the evil giant serpent Apophis; he was considered the son of Bastet. Almost invariably of glazed composition, though a few bronze examples exist, amulets of this deity are characteristic of the Late Period, but a single uncrowned composition example was found in the burial of Hornakht at Tanis.

22 *Nehebkau figures.*
a) Turquoise-blue glazed-composition Nehebkau in the round, standing with its human body supported by a snake's tail. TIP. b) Grey-green glazed-composition flat-backed plaque in raised relief. Nehebkau is carrying offering pots. LP. c) Blue-green glazed-composition Nehebkau in the round, with a snake's tail curled up as a support. H. 5.7 cm, TIP.

23 *Cast bronze animal-headed deities.*
a) Snake-headed figure with gilding, presumably Nehebkau. NK to TIP. b) Lion-headed Mayhes. TIP. c) Seth wearing the Double Crown, with gilding. H. 6.1 cm, Ramesside.

22 The snake god **Nehebkau**, mentioned as early as the *Pyramid Texts*, symbolised invincible living power and became identified with Atum, originally also a chthonic deity; in the *Book of the Dead* Nehebkau acted as one of the forty-two Assessors of the Dead. As an amulet he sometimes appears completely in snake form, uprearing with short upcurled tail tucked in at the back and human arms supporting an extended head. But far more often he is depicted with a human body attached, the end of his snake-form acting like a long tail on which he leans. Both forms are first found in non-royal Third Intermediate Period burials. Virtually the only material used is glazed composition, generally modelled in the round but also moulded with a flat back. One bronze (23a) example of a walking kilted man with a snake's head, which must represent Nehebkau, has gilding on the kilt and wig.

When Osiris became pre-eminent as god of the dead, his brother and murderer **Seth** fell into opprobrium and eventually came to be considered evil personified. Yet originally he too was a member of the ennead (group of nine gods) revered at Heliopolis, although as desert god of storms and aridity he was in constant and unresolved battle with Horus who represented order, civilisation and the fertile Nile Valley. Moreover, Seth never lost his popularity in the delta in spite of being linked by the foreign Hyksos pharaohs with their god Baal; indeed he was the patron god of the Ramesside dynasties, two of whose rulers bore his name. Consequently amulets of Seth can only have (79c) been worn in life as a sign of his patronage and must be little later than the Ramesside Period. A few finely cast bronze examples, some with gilded details, depict him as a man with the head of his sacred animal, as yet unidentified, (23c) with characteristic long curved snout and tall square-topped ears, wearing the White Crown of Upper Egypt, an area which was once unsuccessfully made his domain. However, an extremely unusual glazed-composition amulet of a walking man with a boar's head is unlikely to be a manifestation of Seth, although this animal too came to be associated with evil incarnate. (52b) It probably represents one of the seventy-four forms of the sun-god who is depicted thus in the funerary text *The Litany of the Sun* found in later New Kingdom royal tombs.

Wherever the Nile was rendered treacherous by sandbanks or cliffs or there were marshlands, the crocodile was revered by a kind of propitiatory magic as **Sobk**; thus his main cult sites were at Gebelein, Kom Ombo and in the Faiyum. Although amulets in this form are found even before the beginning of the First Dynasty, they were undoubtedly worn only for an apotropaic reason without any reference to (4d) the god and this probably remained the case for crocodile amulets until the end of dynastic history. Only a crocodile wearing a crown or a sun-disc, or more particularly a man with a crocodile's head, was intended to represent the

24 *Sacred baboons.*
a) Pale turquoise-blue glazed-composition baboon, flat-backed and wearing a full moon and crescent representing Thoth or Khonsu. NK. b) Pale turquoise-blue glazed-composition baboon in the round wearing a *wedjat*-eye on the chest, representing Thoth. H. 3.4 cm, TIP. c) Solid-cast silver and wearing a full moon and crescent. Either Khonsu or Thoth is represented. NK to TIP.

god and such an amulet would have been worn in life as a sign of Sobk's patronage. A finely detailed, tiny cast-gold figure of a crocodile-headed man came from the burial of Hornakht at Tanis; another example wearing a sun-disc thus representing the composite form **Sobk-Re** is probably a little later. Presumably a well-41e modelled glazed-composition crocodile with a falcon's head and sun-disc represents the same composite form.

f, 62a Amulets of **Thoth** in ibis form may have had is, 7e particularly funerary connotations (see page 49), although when ibis-headed, naked and wearing jackal-head slippers he is in his aspect of Hermopolitan creator god. He was also able to assume the shape of a dog-faced baboon, yet even then there are lunar connections, which is why amulets of this type usually wear the full moon and crescent. Baboons, of course, were linked with both the sun and moon. The Egyptians seem to have reasoned that if these animals had foreknowledge of the sun's arrival, 90g which they heralded with screams and paw-waving, they must also have had inside information about the moon's activities. The baboon was the animal form particularly associated with Thoth as inventor of writing and scribe of the gods. Sometimes in the vignette to Chapter 125 of the *Book of the Dead*, depicting the weighing of the heart, it is as baboon that Thoth records the result of the weighing. Sometimes, too, statues of scribes have an image of their patron in this guise squatting beside them or even being carried on their shoulders like St Christopher. Baboon amulets invariably depict the creature with 24 massive mane, squatting with its paws on its knees; in well-modelled examples the sexual member lies prominently between the feet. The moon and crescent are not always on the head, but often the *wedjat*-eye is depicted as a pendant over the chest. The amulet first appears in Ramesside burials, made from glazed composition which continued to be the usual medium. Later, glass formed in an open mould, bronze, silver and some stone were also employed. Presumably such an amulet might be worn in life by a scribe as a sign of his god's patronage.

Before Horus, son of Isis and Osiris, gained importance there were other ancient **falcon-form** gods of the same name, notably Horus of Nekhen, who as patron of Upper Egypt's pre-dynastic capital was the earliest protector of the king, Horus-the-Elder and Horus of Edfu. During the course of the dynastic period the roles and identities of all these like-named gods were constantly being fused, distinguished and reassigned, so that, even with inscriptions, identification is often difficult; for amuletic representations it is almost impossible, especially as the sun god in combination with Horus (see page 29) assumed a falcon's form too.

Horus-the-Elder (in Greek, Haroeris), a primordial creator god whose eyes were the sun and moon, was probably the original opponent of Seth, god of storms and aridity. By the Late Period, however, **Horus of Edfu** (the Behedite) and Horus-the-Elder had become so inextricably associated with a manifestation of **Horus, son of Osiris**, that at Edfu, in the record of the great battle with Seth, the victorious temple god is usually shown in the company of Isis, the mother of his namesake. Both

25 *Falcon deities.*
a) In pale green glazed composition. H. 4.9 cm, TIP. b) In blue-green glazed composition, wearing the triple *atef*. LD. c) In bright turquoise-blue and black glazed composition, wearing a disc on the head. TIP. d) Made in patchy, dark-green glazed composition, wearing the Double Crown, with detailed feathering on the chest only. LD.

25d, 26c 101b, c gods wore the Double Crown and so are probably represented by amulets of falcons and falcon-headed men in the same head-dress. Examples of the crowned falcon amulet in precious metal are found in non-royal burials as early as the Middle Kingdom. In the Third Intermediate Period glazed composition, and later, material such as haematite and chrysoprase, were also employed. Double-crowned falcon-headed men amulets, however, first appear only in royal burials: at Tanis, Hornakht owned a tiny solid-gold seated one and Sheshonq II a standing glazed-composition example wearing a crown made of gold and strung on a gold ribbon. Later, semi-precious stones were used for this type of amulet too: a superb squatting example is carved from obsidian with added gold wig and crown. These amulets would have offered the wearer association with the hero of the Osiris myth and particular protection from the malevolence of Seth. Indeed, one Late Period bronze example depicts the god in the act of harpooning the manifestation of evil. 80b

However, a great number of falcon-headed amulets exist with no head-dress. One of the earliest, squatting and of gold inlaid with lapis lazuli, was around the neck of Tutankhamun's mummy; others, some standing, were found in the Tanis royal burials. Otherwise, amulets of uncrowned falcon-headed men are not found in non-royal burials before the Saite Period, when they are made almost exclusively of lapis lazuli, feldspar and blue glass, and would seem from their position on mummies in close proximity to protagonists in the drama of Osiris to represent one of the forms of his son Horus. Yet there is always the possibility that these squatting mummiform types might represent **Sokaris**, the ancient funerary god of Saqqara. 8c

Uncrowned falcon amulets, of course, first occur in the Old Kingdom: one of the earliest 4f, 67 made in the round from solid gold was a necklace element in a Fourth Dynasty burial at Mostagedda. 67a Thereafter they are found until the end of dynastic history, formed from glazed composition, glass, ivory, bronze, precious metal and every type of semi-precious stone; 25a some superb pieces of Middle and New Kingdom date are of gold cloisonnéwork. Presumably they originally represented a generic Horus with the power to provide their wearer with patronage and protection in this world and the next. 6b Certainly the gold ones may have had a funerary connection, to judge from Chapter 77 of the *Book of the Dead*, which is entitled 'Spell for being transformed into a falcon of gold'. A special form of falcon amulet apparently representing an archaic crouched statue rather than a living bird is found made of bone with characteristic markings in the Predynastic Period; 3a the shape can also be seen atop the gold and turquoise *serekh* beads in the bracelet of the First Dynasty King Djer. 66l Thereafter it occurs sporadically until the end of dynastic history, notably in inlaid gold in the Twenty-second Dynasty burial of Hornakht at Tanis and in a Thirtieth Dynasty non-royal burial at Hawara. There are also some gilded

26 *Falcon-headed deities.*
a) Four figures, presumably the four forms of Monthu, each wearing plumes and sun disc, made in discoloured turquoise-blue glazed composition. H. 3.2 cm, Saite. b) Bright turquoise-blue glazed composition figure wearing a triple *atef*-crown. TIP. c) Pale turquoise-blue glazed-composition deity wearing the Double Crown. TIP to Saite. d) Electrum Khonsu wearing a full and crescent moon and uraeus. TIP. e) Turqoise-blue glazed-composition figure, seated and wearing a sun disc on which a scarab is incised. TIP to Saite.

28e wooden examples of the Roman Period.

The identity of other falcon and falcon-headed amuletic deities is more obvious. In combination with a form of Horus known as 'the horizon dweller', the sun god Re became **Re-Horakhty**, who is represented almost invariably with the sun-disc – and usually the uraeus – on his head. Glazed-composition examples of the falcon wearing the disc first 25c appear in non-royal burials of the Third Intermediate Period; in contemporary royal burials at Tanis, Prince Hornakht owned a superbly detailed tiny solid cast-gold walking falcon-headed Re-Horakhty. Another tiny gold example, found at Defenna in the delta, which rivals it in craftsmanship, still with the plain silver 98b miniature shrine in which it was kept, is probably Twenty-sixth Dynasty in date. This amulet was undoubtedly worn in life as a sign of special devotion to the deity. Thereafter, amulets of the falcon-headed god wearing the sun-disc, both walking and squatting, in the round and in profile, sometimes carrying a *was*-sceptre and *ankh*, almost invariably of glazed composition, occasionally of lapis lazuli and bronze too, are always among the amulets of funerary deities placed on the upper chest of Late Period mummies. They offered their wearer the chance of eternal renewal each morning with the sun. In one unusual seated example in glazed composition, the disc on Re-Horakhty's head is incised with a scarab beetle, 26e an added guarantee of regeneration. However, Re-Horakhty is almost certainly also represented by amulets of a falcon-headed man wearing a triple *atef*-crown, the horns upheld 25b, 26b by an upreared cobra on each shoulder. Superb glazed-composition examples with characteristically attenuated bodies date to the Third Intermediate Period.

For **Horus, Sons of,** *see page 45.*

Monthu was the local Theban war god who was pre-eminent in the area before the arrival of Amun. As an amulet he too is represented as a falcon-headed man, but in metal examples, as a sign of his warlike nature, he carries against his right shoulder the curved sword called a *khepesh*. His usual headgear is two tall plumes 101c with a sun-disc to show his association with the sun god. Sometimes, he appears completely in falcon form, but always wearing his distinctive headgear. More unusual examples include two falcons in tall plumes standing shoulder to 6d shoulder, four falcon-headed figures each wearing double feathers and standing side by 26a side representing the four Monthus (that is, the four main cult centres for the god in the Theban area), and a walking figure with two falcon heads on his shoulders. Although he is bare-headed, the figure carries a *khepesh*, as does another uncrowned single falcon-headed figure. Both amulets must represent Monthu. The only materials employed for amulets of this god appear to be glazed composition and bronze; no examples predate with certainty the Third Intermediate Period.

The **falcon-headed sphinx**, technically a 41d **hieracosphinx**, was also a manifestation of Monthu. Examples of New Kingdom date made from semi-precious stones such as cornelian have inscriptions on the base, and therefore could have served as seals. Unusual glazed-composition examples represent the sphinx seated on its haunches with a large double plume running from ground level behind its back to curve to a stop above the creature's head.

Finally, it should not be forgotten that Khonsu, the Theban moon god, could also take 98c, 26d, the form of a falcon or falcon-headed man, dis- 20c, 13e tinguished from all the foregoing by always wearing the full moon with crescent on his head. A squatting example in limestone dates to the Third Intermediate Period, as may a superbly modelled tiny silver walking falcon-headed man. In the Saite Period and later, glazed composition was the usual material, whether for lunar falcons or walking falcon-headed figures.

The **ram**, revered for its virility and hence 21e its creative powers, was an animal form adopted 66h by more than one deity. It was one guise of **Amen-Re** (the other was a goose) but, in keeping with his late arrival to eminence, the breed was the more recent one with horns curling into the cheeks, not the older breed whose twisted horns project far beyond the head and which was the sacred animal of more than one ancient god. However, possibly for manufacturing reasons, few ram amulets assume the latter form, making identification of the deity depicted more difficult. Indeed, among the many amulets of recumbent or walking rams, invariably of glazed composition or lapis lazuli and mostly of the Saite Period or later, only those which clearly represent a sphinx form (**criosphinx**) with outstretched lion's fore- 55g paws rather than a kneeling ram, or which wear the sun-disc and royal uraeus, can be associated with the king of the gods. One of the finest such amulets from the burial of Wendjebauendjed at Tanis depicts a recumbent ram carved in the round from lapis lazuli and wearing the gold disc and uraeus of Amen-Re. Set in a tall, highly decorated gold base and with a sheet-gold vulture spreading her wings protectively over its lower back, it was kept in a sheet-gold shrine with two suspension loops on the roof and a repoussé ram-sphinx on each long side. A panel at the front slid up to allow the general to look at the amulet whenever he wished. Another lapis lazuli couchant ram-sphinx with a gold snake goddess on its head came from Hornakht's burial at the same site.

Amen-Re's ram-sphinxes were also a popular motif for scarab bases and ring bezels; sometimes the scarab's head itself was replaced 55h, by a ram's. Flat-backed amulets of a ram's head wearing disc and uraeus or uraeus alone and thus representing the king of the gods, made from hollow gold and lapis lazuli as well as 70b glazed composition and frit, were a feature of burials from the Third Intermediate Period onwards. Examples wearing two uraei, of course, suggest a Twenty-fifth Dynasty date. The motif continued to be popular in Meroitic royal jewellery: Amanishakheto owned four solid-gold inlaid shield rings surmounted by 40b rams' heads. Perhaps, then, a contemporary 38e solid-gold ram-headed archer in double plumes, down on one knee to draw his bow, is another aspect of the deity.

At Tanis the burial of Wendjebauendjed also contained a solid-gold amulet of a walking ram-headed man wearing an *atef*-crown, the projecting twisted horns of the headdress resting incongruously above the curled horns of the ram's head. Presumably **Khnum**, the lord of Elephantine at the first cataract, or **Heryshef**, the god of Heracleopolis, is intended, even though both were ancient deities originally represented by the older breed of ram with twisted horns. Khnum was closely connected with the rise of the Nile, heralding the life-bringing inundation, and was often shown creating humankind on a potter's wheel. Heryshef, embodiment of divine majesty, was per-

27 *Ram-headed deities.*
a) Probably Khnum, made in wood and seated on an elaborately decorated throne, wearing the White Crown and carrying an *ankh* in the right hand. H. 7.6 cm, Ramesside. b) Lapis-lazuli, flat, double-sided squatting figure. TIP. c) Pale turquoise-blue glazed-composition figure seated on a decorated throne and wearing an *atef*-crown, holding an *ankh* in the right hand and a *was* in the left with the shaft lying down the left leg. TIP.
d) Dark Egyptian blue ram's head in tripartite wig wearing an *atef*-crown and surmounting a papyrus column on a stand. LD.

haps a primordial creator god; his chief cult place was the capital for two dynasties of rulers during the First Intermediate Period, at which time he became strongly associated with Osiris. The *atef*-crowned ram-headed deity is also found as a glazed-composition amulet in a squatting posture and seated. We can be almost certain that Khnum rather than Heryshef is represented only when, as in a wooden example, he wears the White Crown of Upper Egypt. However, mummies of Twenty-sixth and Thirtieth Dynasty date occasionally wore over their chests glazed-composition walking ram-headed amulets without a head-dress: it is impossible to tell whether they were intended to evoke Khnum for his powers of (re)creation or Heryshef because of his Osirian connection.

27c
27a
20d

During the Third Intermediate Period non-royal burials began to contain amulets of well-modelled walking rams, sometimes with heavy fleeces but always without a head-dress, made from glazed composition; later lapis lazuli and glass were used too. Only a sheet-gold example with incised details is able, because of the medium, to distinguish the older breed with long twisted horns, suggesting that an ancient deity is represented. However, a chalcedony ram resting its body on a seemingly grossly enlarged tail must depict the newer breed whose other feature is curled horns, unless a fat ram-headed crocodile is what is really intended. By the Late Period a kneeling, possibly mummiform ram amulet, almost exclusively of glazed composition, is even more popular, and a few examples wear the *atef*. Five hundred years earlier at Tanis, Wendjebauendjed was buried with an amulet comprising a polished-stone shaft surmounted by a gold ram's head also in an *atef*, the whole flanked by two *djed*-pillars, suggesting that the deity in question was **Banebdjedet**, the ancient ram god of Mendes in the delta. There is no doubt that some of the Late Period ram amulets were intended to represent this deity: whether walking or mummiform, they have four heads, two facing frontwards and two backwards. As early as the Ramesside Period this was the method of symbolising this god's four manifestations as Soul (*Ba*) of Re, Shu, Geb and Osiris. Perhaps, then, some of the other rams should be linked with Banebdjedet too.

28g
28a
64i, 27d
41f

28 *Sacred animals.* From LEFT to RIGHT
a) Pale turquoise-blue glazed-composition recumbent ram. Saite. b) Pale green glazed-composition finger-ring with a papyrus-head at one end of the shank surmounted by shrew mouse, sacred to Horus of Letopolis. H. of ring 3.5 cm, TIP. c) Pale green glazed-composition hippopotamus standing on a reed mat. TIP or later. d) Gilded wood vulture of Nekhbet or Mut. G-R. e) Gilded wood archaic crouched falcon. G-R. f) Black-and-white diorite seated cat of Bastet. H. 1.8 cm, TIP. g) Bluish chalcedony kneeling fat-tailed ram (or ram-headed crocodile) of Amun. NK to TIP. h) Diorite squatting frog, sacred to Heqat. NK to TIP.

A god who is always depicted in human form is **Atum**, one of the aspects of the sun god, yet as amulet he appears only in his animal manifestation of a **lizard**, noted for its love of sunshine. Small bronze reliquaries with suspension loop surmounted by one or more basking reptiles (and containing a lizard mummy or part of a mummy) are characteristic of the Late Period, worn as a sign of special devotion to the god. Contemporary glazed-composition lizards on plaques might have had a similar purpose.

48d

28b

The **shrew-mouse** with its long pointed muzzle, short legs and long tail, always depicted walking, was the animal manifestation of the form of **Horus** called 'the blind and seeing god', worshipped at Letopolis in the delta. Since the creature lives underground, thus symbolising the god's blind aspect, its re-emergence into the sunlight was a metaphor for rebirth. Thus anyone wearing a small bronze amulet of the shrew-mouse, all of Late Period date, would be offered the same opportunity of enjoying resurrection.

Female Animal-Headed and Animal Deities

Of all the maned lion goddesses who were revered for their fierceness **Bastet** alone was 'transmogified' into the less terrible cat, although even she often retained a lion-head when depicted as a woman, thus causing much confusion in identification. The female cat was particularly noted for its fecundity and so Bastet was adored as goddess of fertility and, with rather less obvious logic, of festivity and intoxication. This is why, as a cat-headed woman, she carries a *menyet* collar with *aegis*-capped counterpoise and rattles a sistrum, both musical instruments connected with merry-making, but she nearly always has kittens near at hand as evidence of her fertility, occasionally carried in the round-bottomed basket which can hang over her arm. Such figures are invariably of cast metal and depict Bastet in a highly patterned full-length dress; she never wears a head-dress. Very few, however, were intended to be worn as amulets: most are far too large and heavy and were provided with a plinth so that the piece might be set up as a votive figure.

28f

Usually Bastet as amulet assumes the shape of a cat; some small metal seated cats with a

29 *Cats of Bastet.*
a) Made of rock crystal, and seated. NK.
b) Blue-green glazed-composition cat seated on a papyrus column. TIP. c) Blue-green glazed-composition cat, seated with a kitten between her legs. TIP. d) Turquoise-blue glazed-composition cat with black spotting. She is seated with eight kittens plus one on her back and one on her head. H. 4.5 cm, TIP.

loop on the spine were obviously worn with this purpose. However, one of the best-known representations of the goddess as a reclining cat with kittens in a row at her teats or touching her face, usually of cast bronze, was never intended as an amulet. Instead cat-form amulets of Bastet are most often formed in the round from glazed composition, a variety of semi-precious stones and some precious metal, and depict her seated alone or with kittens. (29) Sometimes the kittens just lean up her front legs or she rests a paw across their necks. In a particularly elaborate type, however, Bastet sits with her front legs supported horizontally on the heads of four outward-facing seated kittens, two more sit at the front and two perch on her paws, making eight in all; one or more others sit on her head! Amulets in the shape of a glazed-composition papyrus column surmounted by one or more seated cats are of unclear significance unless they symbolise a syncretistic form of Bastet and Wadjyt, (29b) the papyrus serving as a punning reference to the latter's name.

Crudely shaped but unmistakable cat-form amulets first appear in late Old Kingdom burials made from glazed composition and bone; perhaps already they represent the goddess, otherwise they must have been intended to endow their wearer with fertility. During the New Kingdom, often carved from semi-precious stones such as cornelian, they served as ring bezels (45j) or formed the backs of scaraboids. In one pair of gold-ribbed penannular earrings a tiny cat would have lain against the wearer's ear. The elaborate glazed-composition types with numerous kittens, or comprising a column, do not occur before the Third Intermediate Period. All such pieces must have been worn by women to place them under the patronage of the goddess and perhaps endow them with her fecundity. (6a) They were essentially to be worn in life, but could also have potency in the Other World.

Amuletic cats formed a part of the insignia of royal ladies of the early New Kingdom too. Three cast-gold examples recline on each of the two bracelet spacer bars of Queen Sobkemsaf, (48b) wife of the Seventeenth Dynasty ruler Nubkheperre Inyotef. Each of the wives of Tuthmosis III once wore a bead bracelet with a spacer-bar surmounted by five reclining cats of gold, cornelian and composition. Gold-foil seated cats are also a component of the openwork amuletic collar of Queen Aahhotep.

The numerous amulets of maned **lion-headed women** which first appear in and are a feature of the Third Intermediate Period, walking and seated, with and without insignia, (8a, b, 64l,) usually made of finely modelled glazed composition though occasionally of precious metal, lapis lazuli and sard, are among the most difficult to identify; even the few with inscriptions tend to give contradictory information. One type, usually of two-coloured glaze, depicts the goddess bare-headed, holding a detailed sistrum (30a, d) on her knee and seated on an elaborate openwork throne whose sides are almost invariably formed from the sinuous body of the

30 *Lion-headed goddesses.*
a) Turquoise-blue and black glazed-composition figure, seated on an openwork throne with Nehebkau on the sides, holding a hoop-shaped sistrum. TIP. b) Pale turquoise-blue glazed-composition figure, walking and holding a lion-headed *aegis* to her chest. TIP. c) Grass-green glazed-composition goddess, walking, wearing a uraeus, and holding a *wedjat*-eye to her chest. The back-pillar names Bastet. H. 7.6 cm, TIP. d) Turquoise-blue and black glazed-composition goddess, seated on an openwork throne with Nehebkau on the sides, holding a shrine-shaped sistrum. TIP.

snake god Nehebkau. The sistrum suggests that Bastet in her original fearsome form is represented. Figures with a tall upreared cobra 30b, c on top of the head which forms the front of the suspension loop, sometimes carrying a papyrus sceptre, *wedjat*-eye or *menyet* counterpoise surmounted by an *aegis*, are occasionally actually named as Bastet. Yet sometimes, too, identical figures are identified as **Sekhmet**, the fierce goddess of the Memphite area, who symbolised the burning heat of the sun and, as the sun-god's vengeful eye, destroyed his enemies and brought plague and pestilence. Rather inappropriately, she was made the wife 13b, d of Ptah and mother of Nefertum to form a local sacred family. It might be thought that Sekhmet is probably represented by those 9b, 101c figures with a sun-disc on the head, for they 40a, c, e have an obvious solar connection. However, identical large-scale votive bronzes specifically name **Wadjyt**, the protectress of Lower Egypt, who usually assumed the form of the cobra (as when worn on pharaoh's forehead next to Nekhbet, the vulture protectress of Upper Egypt). In addition, two of the finest cast-gold pendant amulets from Wendjebauendjed's burial at Tanis, depicting a superbly modelled walking lion-headed woman with detailed jewellery, wearing sun-disc and tall uraeus, is specifically named as Bastet. From the same source and with the same identity is a rather unusual rock-crystal figure with added gold disc and uraeus, seated on a throne decorated with inlaid sheet gold and wire-work.

Amulets of lion-headed women wearing the Double Crown represent a fusion of Sekhmet with the Theban goddess **Mut** (see page 22). In one example she suckles not the sacred child 19c but a fully-grown king carrying a crook. In another she stands to offer her breast to a naked child who is too small to reach; a second god- 19a dess stands at her back, her wings enveloping them all. Figures wearing cow's horns and disc with double feathers have been identified as **Mehyt**, a local goddess of the Abydos area, but one example at least is specifically named as Mut. This still leaves a considerable number of amulets of lion-headed women without a head-dress or distinguishing feature. A few rare examples, however, who stand on the prostrate figures of captives can only be **Pakhet**, the local goddess of Beni Hasan, to whom a whole cemetery of cat mummies was devoted during the Late Period. There can be little doubt that all these amulets were worn in life as a sign of patronage, protection and, perhaps, with a hope for fecundity (see also **Aegis**, page 41).

Wadjyt, as protectress of Lower Egypt, most often assumed the guise of a **cobra**, but she was

31 *Protective female deities.*
a) Pale green glazed-composition female-headed snake wearing a tripartite wig. Saite. b) Lion-headed Thoeris in pale Egyptian blue. H. 5.9 cm, from Saqqara. LD. c) Pale turquoise-blue glazed-composition female-headed Thoeris wearing a tripartite wig; perhaps Ipet is intended. NK to TIP. d) Pale green glazed-composition cow-headed snake, perhaps Isis-Hathor, wearing horns, disc and plumes. H. 6.2 cm, Saite.

just one of the goddesses to do so. Possibly only those amulets in the form of a papyrus column (*wadj*) surmounted by an upreared snake are to be identified with her by a linguistic pun on her name; examples in gilded wood and flat-backed glazed composition and glass dating to the Late Period are known. However, if the cobra wears the White Crown, **Nekhbet** is represented, the protectress of Upper Egypt, who was usually depicted as a vulture. There are, in addition, cobra amulets with the head of a cat, lion, cow or woman. Some are large and well modelled in the round from glazed composition, others are small and roughly made from flat-backed moulded composition or glass; a few are of lapis lazuli. Except for a sheet-gold example from the burial of Tutankhamun none appears to predate the Saite Period. The cat-headed cobra must be **Bastet**; a relief actually names a lion-headed example Sekhmet, Wadjyt and Tefnut! The cow's head wears the horns, disc and feathers of **Hathor**, although by the Late Period she and **Isis** are often almost indistinguishable. The cobra with woman's head sometimes wears the low round crown also associated with Isis, but on other occasions the Double Crown of **Mut** or the two plumes which link her with **Renenutet**, the harvest goddess, nurse and protectress of pharaoh. Tutankhamun's gold example wearing feathers horns and disc and depicted suckling the young king is actually named Weret-hekau, unfortunately the epithet of more than one goddess, including Mut.

41c

31d

31a

The sky goddess whose arched body formed the vault of heaven gave birth to the sun each dawn and swallowed him each dusk; conversely, she bore the myriad stars each evening and gobbled them up each dawn. It is not surprising that, as mother of the stars, she should have taken the form of a great **sow**, for the female pig's habit of eating her own piglets must have been well known. Glazed-composition amulets of a vast rooting sow, either walking alone or with up to seven piglets marching between her legs, first occur in Third Intermediate Period burials. Many bear an inscription naming the goddess as **Nut** but others call her Isis, evidence of the latter's takeover in all matters of divine motherhood. Perhaps this duality is represented in those examples which have a head at each end. Such amulets were intended to endow their wearer with fecundity.

32

For **Thoeris** *see page 40.*

32 *The sky-goddess as a sow.*
a) Blue-green glazed-composition figure modelled with piglets symbolising the stars. L. 5.4 cm, Saite. b) Pale blue-green glazed-composition goddess, double-headed and modelled, perhaps representing the sky-goddess' dual aspect as Nut-Isis. TIP.

3

Amulets for Protection and Aversion

Petrie termed the amulets intended to give protection 'phylactic', but in the same category must be included those which worked apotropaically, representing the very danger to be warded off.

Animate Forms

Such is certainly the symbolism of the hobbled 3b shell **hippopotamus** found in a Badarian burial and thus the earliest representational amulet from Egypt, for it shows the beast incapacitated. Perhaps the early **hippopotamus head** amulet had a similar function: to ward off the greatly feared beast it depicted. Yet grazing hippopotamus amulets in semi-precious stones, of Middle Kingdom date, just like contemporary large glazed-composition examples, 69b, 4a seem peaceful. A **turtle** amulet, at any rate, 67g was undoubtedly intended to work apotropaically, for it was a creature of evil symbolising death and darkness. Perhaps because of its water-based existence, it was believed, like the evil serpent Apophis, to inhabit the murky waters of the Underworld, waiting to impede the nightly progression of the sun god's barque. It was certainly considered his arch-enemy: 'May Re live and the turtle die,' as New Kingdom coffin inscriptions and some contemporary tomb texts demand. In Late Period temples the turtle is depicted being harpooned, and thus rendered harmless, just as often as the hippopotamus, that other symbol of malevolence. Turtle amulets are made from such varied materials as green- or blue-glazed composition, amethyst, ivory, serpentine, moulded hollow sheet-gold and, in particular, cornelian, olivine and green jasper. There are two distinct forms: one naturalistically represents the head, legs and tail emerging from the shell, the other is little more than a convex disc with a protruding head.

Amulets in the shape of the **scorpion**, made 4k from glazed composition, ivory and bone, first appear as early as the Fifth Dynasty, and at so early a date the probability is that they were worn as apotropaic protection against this noxious reptile's sting. Certainly on *cippi* (see 34, page 38) and in Late Dynastic magical texts the scorpion is always the chief creature against which spells are directed. Although scorpion amulets continued to be made until the Ptolemaic Period, in glass too, the strangely ambiguous attitude the Egyptians held towards dangerous creatures allowed the scorpion goddess **Serqet** to be revered at exactly the same 20e time as a protectress of the dead.

The **crocodile** possessed a similar duality. 4d Known in amuletic form even before the First Dynasty, it does not appear in numbers until the late Old Kingdom, usually made of glazed composition, either pierced through its length or with a suspension loop. It continued to be produced, sometimes from stone as well, throughout the Dynastic Period. In the developed form the long snout is held up by a support and the space beneath served for suspension. In scaraboids of New Kingdom date two crocodiles in the round curve into a 54e circle to form the back, the tail of one under the head of the other; the underside often depicts two more crocodiles in sunken relief. Glazed-composition examples of Saite date exist in which as many as seven finely modelled rep- 93g

33 *Hybrid-form protective divine powers.*
a) Pale blue-green glazed-composition baboon, with bird's wings and tail, wearing an *atef*-crown. LP. b) Pale green glazed-composition upreared cobra body, with lion legs and a crocodile tail, two forward-facing ape heads and two backward-facing Bes heads. H. 7.6 cm, LP. c) Pale blue-green glazed-composition dwarf's body with a ram's head, bird's wings and tail, wearing full and crescent moons with a uraeus. LP.

tiles stretch out side by side on top of a plaque. Without doubt these amuletic forms were intended to act apotropaically: the Egyptians were so frightened of the crocodile in life that some of the spells on *cippi* were directed specifically against it; moreover, if it ate its victims, it denied them an Afterlife. Even in the Other World it was dangerous: Chapters 31 and 32 of the *Book of the Dead* were expressly aimed at repelling a crocodile 'which comes to steal the deceased's magic'. Yet at the same time the crocodile was deified and worshipped under the name **Sobk** – the theory was that if this dangerous creature was thus propitiated, it would do no harm. Moreover, the crocodile was a symbol of rebirth, for it lived in the reincarnating waters of the primordial ocean into which it sank and from which it rose like the sun.

Standing vultures made from ivory, bone, copper and glazed composition are first found in late Old Kingdom burials; two thousand years later no fewer than eight were illustrated among prescribed funerary amulets in the MacGregor list. Five sheet-gold vultures were at the throat of Tutankhamun's mummy; at Tanis, Hornakht owned three with inlays, Wendjebauendjed four and Amenemope one of sheet gold with incised details. The latter type continued to be placed on non-royal mummies of the Twenty-sixth Dynasty; later still they were made of gilded wood or glass, sometimes polychrome. Although for the dead such amulets would always have an underlying apotropaic function – vultures were very dangerous to any corpse – they undoubtedly became associated with the protective vulture goddesses such as **Nekhbet** (see Chapter 2). In the MacGregor Papyrus one is named Weret-hekau (Great of Magic), an epithet of the goddess Mut among others.

16b

28d

What might be expected to be apotropaic are curious monstrous **hybrid figures** in the round, which are characteristic of the Late Period. Made from well-modelled glazed composition, they have dwarf-like bodies and bandy legs, a non-human head and full, closed birds' wings behind. Some are ram-headed with horns curled into the cheeks, wearing an *atef*-crown or even a crescent and full moon; others have the head of a dog-faced baboon, also wearing an *atef*. The suspension loop is usually behind the shoulders, but occasionally behind the crown. It cannot be a coincidence that similar creatures but with multiple heads are depicted in the vignettes of contemporary magical papyri where the text indicates that

33

34 *Cippus amulets.*
a) Pale green glazed-composition *pataikos* with a scarab on the head flanked by Isis and Nephthys holds snakes and stands on crocodiles. TIP. b) Dark green glazed-composition *pataikos* in *atef*, holding knives and standing on crocodiles. H. 7.8 cm, TIP. c) Pale green glazed-composition naked figure wearing a Bes mask, with multiple winged arms holding emblems of power. The figure stands on a tail-eating ouroboros snake above a plinth encircled by figures of noxious creatures –crocodile, wolf, scorpion, turtle and snakes. LP.

they represent the power of a deity 'whose great and mysterious forms are usually hidden from gods and men'. In other words they represent not evil but divine power personified and are capable of overwhelming any menacing opposing forces, whether human or divine, in this world or the next.

Interestingly enough, some contemporary superbly modelled green-glazed composition amulets depict in the round one of Egypt's most instantly recognisable protective genies, the leonine-featured Bes, in a form almost indistinguishable from that in one of the magical papyrus vignettes. In the best examples he is naked, frontal-faced, wears double plumes, horns and disc; multiple animal heads flank each side of his head and in three of his four hands he holds a *was*-sceptre. The high oval plinth on which he stands, in his jackal-head slippers, is encircled by the tail-swallowing *ouroboros* snake and by a frieze of noxious animals including the crocodile, lion, snake, turtle, jackal, hippopotamus and scorpion. His large double wings are outstretched and, at the back, tail and back feathers are carefully delineated. 34c, 35c

These amulets are undoubtedly a variant of that most protective of amuletic forms the ***cippus***, a plaque against which is set a raised-relief standing figure of Horus-the-Child, the saviour, with the head of Bes above him, grasping and standing on all manner of biting, stinging and harmful creatures. Every surface front and back is covered with scenes and texts designed to give protection by magical means from the bite and sting of the noxious creatures depicted (all of which are shown on the plinth on which the Bes figures stand). On 34a, b 35a, b

35 *Reverse of cippus amulets, above.*
a and b) Winged goddesses, each wearing a sun disc, stand on crocodiles to protect *pataikos*' back.
b) Is a lion-headed goddess.
c) The bird's wings and tail feathers of the mask-wearing human figure seen on the front, show links with hybrid protective powers. LP.

the other hand, most *cippi* are of stone and are often quite substantial objects. Indeed, it is known that they were set up in temple precincts so that water might be poured over them to absorb the magic of their scenes and spells; when drunk, the water would afford prophylactic protection against the creatures in question or perhaps cure those already bitten or stung. However, glazed-composition *cippi* also exist, as do small stone examples complete with means of suspension, indicating that they must have been worn.

Yet another variant of the protective *cippus* motif appears in glazed composition amulets of the Third Intermediate Period and later, depicting in the round the naked dwarf god 36 ***pataikos*** standing on crocodiles and strangling snakes (which he sometimes also appears to be eating) or brandishing knives. Bronze examples are also known. Lest there be any doubt of his connection with Horus-the-Saviour, he is usually flanked by the standing figures of Isis and Nephthys. A falcon perches on each shoulder, a scarab clings to his bald head and a winged goddess, sometimes with a lion's head wearing a disc, spreads out her wings protectively behind him; occasionally it is the lotus god Nefertum who guards his back. These substantial amulets always have a hole for suspension behind the dwarf's head.

The *pataikoi* are named from a passage in the writings of Herodotus describing Phoenician dwarf-form protective images. Perhaps they represent a form of Ptah as craftsman god, for dwarfs are always present among the workers in precious-metal workshops in Old Kingdom scenes of daily life. In the past they have been called Ptah-Seker figures, linking them with the falcon-form Memphite funerary god. The *pataikos* appears as an amulet in his own right as early as the Sixth Dynasty (if that is how a considerable number of extremely crude glazed-composition figures are indeed to be interpreted), but it is not until the New Kingdom that recognisable examples made in an open-backed mould first occur. The finest pieces, however, so finely modelled in the round that they appear almost sculpted, date to the Third Intermediate Period and later. Although the *pataikos* always assumes the slightly crouched posture of Bes, a number of variant details have been identified. Often the head is bare or surmounted by the two plumes and disc or an elaborate *atef*-crown with pendant uraei, or a simple side-lock is worn. The figure may be falcon-headed or ram-headed, in the latter case with the head set backwards on the shoulders; sometimes the figure is two-headed like Janus. In other instances there are two complete figures set back to back: one is the *pataikos*, the other Bes or a falcon-headed dwarf.

36 *Protective* pataikoi. a) Pale turquoise-blue glazed-composition *pataikos* with cropped hair. LD, from Saqqara. b) Turquoise-blue and black glazed-composition *pataikos* with a scarab on its head, eating snakes, brandishing knives and standing on crocodiles. There are protective signs on the underside of the base. H. 8.4 cm, TIP, from Matmar.

Bes too, of course, occurs in amuletic form in his own right as early as the Eighteenth Dynasty, although his image is found far earlier, notably on ivory magic wands of Middle Kingdom date where he brandishes snakes in the company of other protective beings. He is instantly recognisable, for, almost alone in Egyptian art, he is depicted full-faced and a complete lion's mane surrounds very leonine

37 *Bes figures.*
a) Grey-green glazed-composition squatting Bes in the round, wearing plumes. H. 2.8 cm, LP, from Tell Nebesha. b) Bes of turquoise-blue glazed composition, in the round, lacking a mane but wearing plumes. H. 5.2 cm, LP. c) Grass-green glazed-composition, flat-backed figure carrying a drum and holding his tail. NK. d) Turquoise-blue glazed-composition Bes in the round, wearing plumes. TIP.

features; significantly he has a lion's tail. Always naked, dwarf-like with bandy legs, and wearing tall plumes, Bes usually rests his hands on his hips. In Graeco-Roman Period examples, however, he sometimes carries a round shield and brandishes a sword as tangible evidence of his protective qualities, for Bes was a genie who warded off evil influences at childbirth. He was a deity for whom there were no temples, but the numbers in which his images occur indicate his great popularity throughout the later Dynastic Period. His amulets are most often made of glazed composition, sometimes polychrome, very occasionally of cornelian and glazed steatite too, all modelled in the round; in the Late Period solid cast-bronze examples also occur. The burial of the wives of Tuthmosis III contained a bracelet partly composed of hollow gold Bes pendants stamped into a mould with back-plate added; usually, though, flat-backed examples are of glazed composition or glass made in an open-backed mould. Sometimes in the New Kingdom Bes is depicted in profile beating a drum or tambourine, for he was closely connected with music-making; indeed it was this noisy activity which was believed to drive away malevolent forces.

37 | 6c | 37c

From the Third Intermediate Period onwards Bes heads alone occur as an amulet, often with sharp teeth showing and tongue poking out. They are usually moulded with a flat back from glazed composition or glass, or modelled in high relief on a plaque or disc, in which case the other side might carry an equally protective *wedjat*. Characteristic of the same period are finger-rings of bright-blue-glazed composition; these are of openwork wedding-band type for which a popular motif is a column of Bes figures, each standing on another's shoulders.

15a, d | 45e

Amulets of Bes were particularly worn in life, especially by women and children, but they served a protective purpose just as well in the tomb, as did those in the shape of the goddess whom he aided as she attended women at the moment of childbirth, the hippopotamus **Thoeris** (in Egyptian Taweret). The female river horse, however, was a form also assumed by **Ipet**, who provided heat and light for the dead, so there is always the possibility that she is the deity actually represented.

The different attitude the Egyptians held towards the male and female of a species when both were deified is very evident in the hippopotamus. As has been seen, the male was the embodiment of evil while the female was invariably benevolent, although she bares fearsome teeth and sports a crocodile's tail. Why she became linked with childbirth is not at all clear. It has been noticed, though, that in the upright posture she assumes, her breasts are pendulous and her stomach swollen, like those of a pregnant woman. A feather headdress, low cylindrical modius or horns and disc are usually worn, often her stumpy forelegs lean for support on a protective *sa*-sign or *ankh*, or brandish a knife. Thoeris amulets occur as early as the late Old Kingdom and were made throughout the Dynastic Period. Blue- or green-glazed composition modelled in the round or moulded with a flat back is by far the commonest material, but glazed steatite, lapis

39

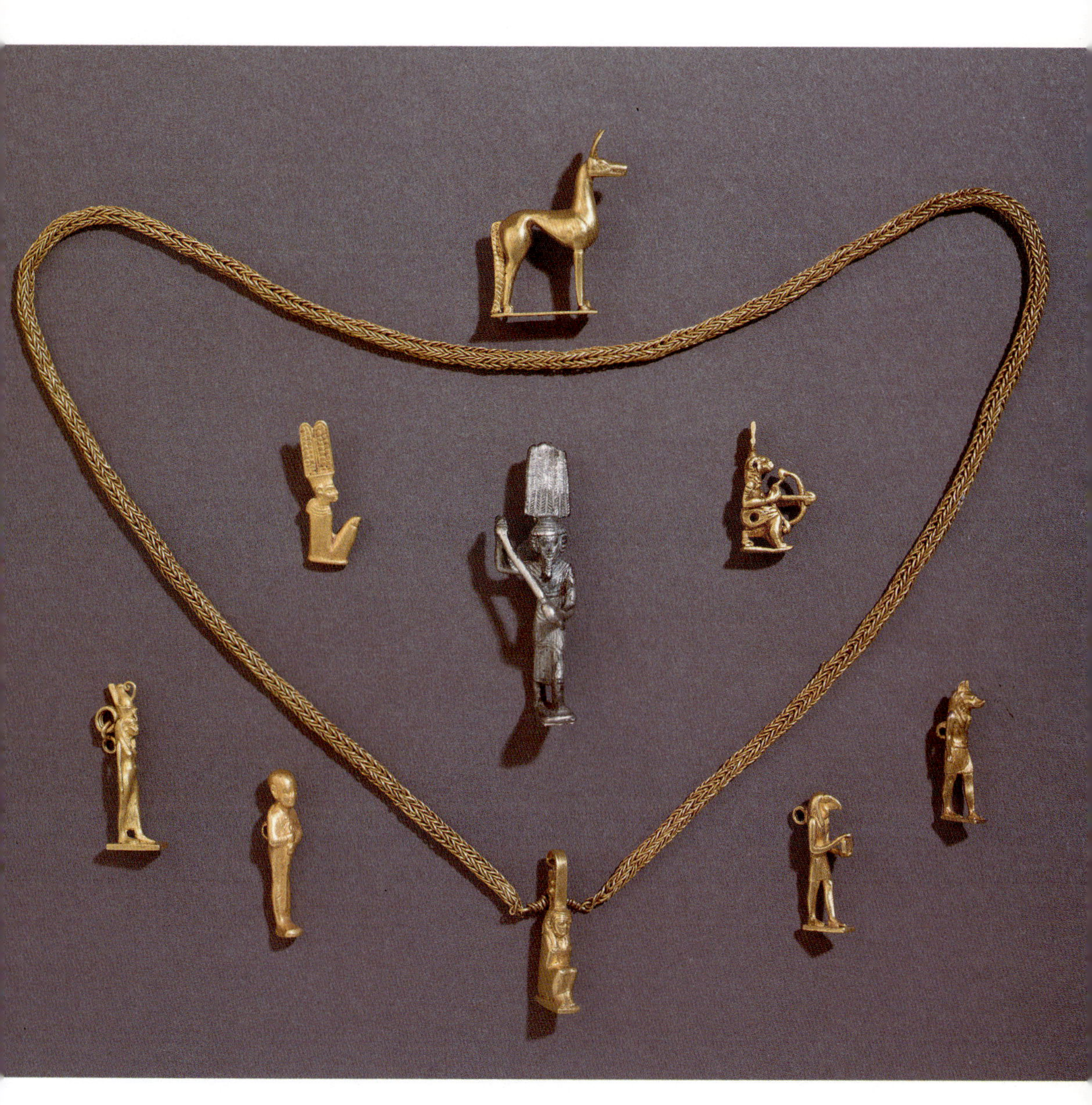

38 *Precious metal deities.*
From the TOP, LEFT TO RIGHT a) Solid-cast gold wolf (?), perhaps Wepwawet, protector of Osiris. H. 3–1 cm; Meroitic. b) Gold foil Maat on a loop-in-loop gold chain, perhaps a judge's insignia. Saite or later. c) Sheet gold, flat-backed, squatting Amen-Re, king of the gods. LD. d) Warrior god Inhert in solid-cast silver in the act of hurling his lance. H. 4.8 cm; TIP. e) Solid-cast gold ram-headed kneeling archer in double plumes, perhaps a form of Amen-Re. Meroitic. f) Solid-cast gold Mut, wife of Amen-Re. H. 2.9 cm; NK to TIP. g) Solid-cast gold Ptah, creator god of Memphis. LD. h) Ibis-headed Thoth in solid-cast gold returning the *wedjat* eye. TIP. i) Solid-cast gold jackal-headed Anubis, god of embalming. TIP.

39 ABOVE *Thoeris*.
a) Glazed-composition, flat-backed Thoeris, wearing a low modius, resting on a *sa* and holding a knife. H. 7.8 cm, NK. b) Glazed-composition three-dimensional figure with hands turned down as though resting on a support. H. 5.2 cm, TIP. c and d) Glazed steatite figures, flat-backed with two heads. NK. e) Glazed composition, in the round, wearing low modius, horns and disc. NK. f) Glazed-composition Thoeris, flat-backed, with a human body. LD.

40 Aegis *and counterpoise*.
a) Glazed-composition counterpoise, its lion-headed *aegis* wearing a disc and uraeus above Bes grasping cobras. *Wedjat*-eye in the roundel. b) Flat-backed jasper *aegis*, its ram's head wearing disc and cobra which in turn wears horns and disc. Pectoral with scarab on the chest. H. 3.5 cm. c) Glazed-composition counterpoise, its lion-headed *aegis* in disc and uraeus, above Nehebkau. In the roundel Horus-the-Child sits on a lotus flanked by winged cobras and *ba*. The underside has a rosette.
d) Bronze counterpoise with Shu and lion-headed Tefnut above seated solar lion-headed deity. Roundel has a *Barbus* sacred to Mehyt. e) Sheet silver *aegis*; its solid-cast solar lion's head, flanked by falcon heads, wears a *wedjat*-eye.
f) Glazed-composition pendulum-shaped two-sided counterpoise topped by the head of Mut in vulture wig. H. 11.7 cm.

41 ABOVE *Hybrid-forms.*
a) Lapis lazuli human-headed vulture, its long hair with a central parting. MK. b) Flat-backed glazed-composition falcon-headed fly wearing full moon and crescent, a *wedjat*-eye over the wings. Late TIP. c) Lapis lazuli cat-headed cobra. H. 2.5 cm; LD. d) Cornelian falcon-headed sphinx-form Monthu; the underside names Ramesses II. 19th Dynasty. e) Glazed-composition falcon-headed crocodile wearing sun disc. L. 3.6 cm; Saite. f) Lapis lazuli ram with four heads representing the forms of Banebdjedet of Mendes. LP.

42 *Cylinder amulets.*
a) Hollow gold cylinder with removable cap and granulation on the shaft. It would once have contained a papyrus written with a spell to protect women and children. H. 7.3 cm, 12th Dynasty. b) Amethyst beads alternate with gold foil over a core to form a solid cylinder with caps, imitating a hollow example. 12th Dynasty. c) Amethyst beads alternate with gold foil over a core to form a solid dummy-capped cylinder. H. 4.6 cm, 12th Dynasty.

45 ABOVE *Amuletic finger-rings.*
FROM LEFT TO RIGHT a) Gold ring with swivelling bezel, a plain amethyst scarab. L. of scarab 1.6 cm, 12th Dynasty. b) Glazed-composition lion-headed *aegis* wearing a sun disc, above a lotus flower. Part of the shank is formed by the counterpoise. H. 3.5 cm, TIP, from Matmar. c) Glazed-composition *aegis* of Mut wearing the Double Crown and surmounting a papyrus-head. The counterpoise forms part of the shank. TIP. d) Gold ring with a swivelling bezel, a plain obsidian scarab. 12th Dynasty, from Abydos. e) Glazed-composition openwork ring with a column of Bes figures standing on each others' heads. TIP. f) Ring with solar falcon-headed gods seated around an *ankh* and Hathor. Openwork, glazed-composition. H. 2.8 cm, TIP. g) Glazed-composition openwork ring with an *aegis* of Bastet. TIP. h) Gold ring with swivelling bezel decorated with granulation surmounted by a solid-cast frog. The underside is incised with a scorpion. 18th Dynasty. i) Solid gold ring. The bezel has a scene of Mut enthroned in a barque. NK. j) Gold ring with a swivelling bezel, a cornelian cat on a plinth. The underside bears an *ankh* sign. 18th Dynasty.

43 ABOVE LEFT *Protective amulets.*
a) A pair of gold fish (*nekhau*) inlaid with feldspar, a charm against drowning. MK. b) Gold trussed ducks, wallet beads, a snake's head and lotus flower. 18th Dynasty. c) A pair of gold fish inlaid with quartz and chalcedony. L. 3.6 cm, MK. d) Electrum oyster shell to give health. MK. e) (Surrounding the rest). Hollow gold Thoeris amulets with long gold beads. L. of amulets 1.8 cm, 18th Dynasty.

44 LEFT *Heart scarabs.*
a) Steatite, very flat, human-headed heart scarab. The underside bears Chapter 30B of the *Book of the Dead* for the woman Isis. L. 6.8 cm, NK. b) The scarab's underside has Chapter 30B of the *Book of the Dead* for the priest of Amun Pa-di-Atum. Green basalt. LD. c) The underside has incised Chapter 30B of the *Book of the Dead* for the Chief Administrator of Neith Wahibre-mer-Neith, born to Takernet. Green marble. Saite. d) Green glazed steatite scarab inlaid with blue glass and cornelian. The underside bears Chapter 30B of the *Book of the Dead* but a name has not been inserted in the space for it. NK. e) Green glazed-composition scarab, whose underside has Chapter 30B of the *Book of the Dead* for a person whose name was never filled in. TIP. f) Green basalt scarab with gold foil remaining around legs. The underside bears Chapter 30B of the *Book of the Dead* for the woman Semast, born to Renpet-nefer. Saite. g) Green jasper human-headed scarab. The underside has Chapter 30B of the *Book of the Dead* for the High Steward Nebankh, who served king Sobkhotep IV. L. 3.1 cm, 13th Dynasty (*c.*1710 BC).

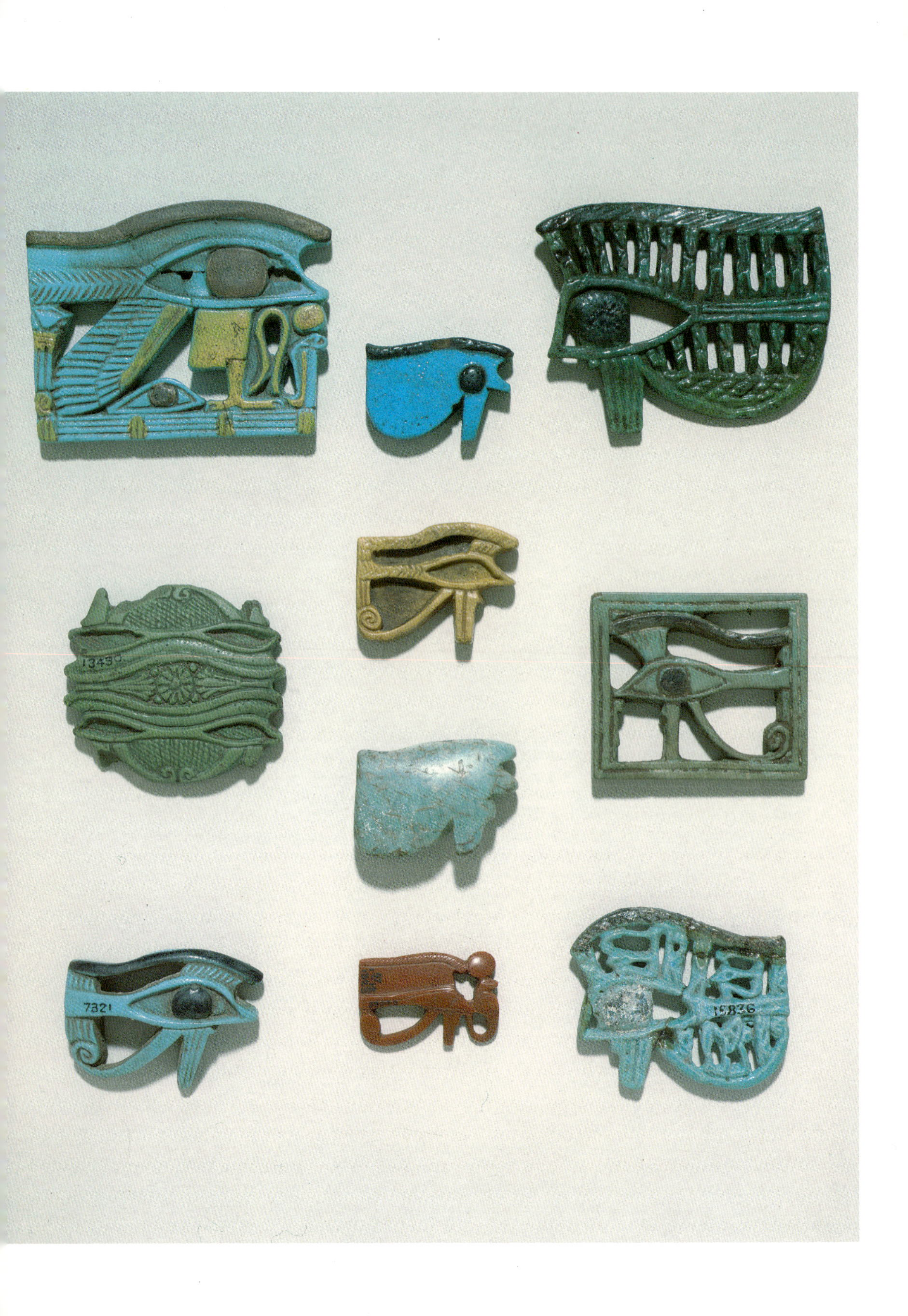
7321
15836

47 ABOVE Polychrome glazed-composition pylon-shaped pectoral with incorporated heart scarab in a barque, blessed by Isis and Nephthys and flanked by a Girdle Tie of Isis and a *djed*. The underside of the scarab bears Chapter 30B of the *Book of the Dead* – the heart scarab formula – for a woman called Ptahemheb. H. 9.7 cm, probably from Memphis. 19th Dynasty.

46 LEFT *Wedjat*-eyes.
FROM LEFT TO RIGHT a) Polychrome, glazed-composition openwork eye with plain back, the drop and spiral turned into a falcon's leg and wing. Added human eye and uraeus; standing on a reed mat. W. 6.7 cm, TIP. b) Two-tone, glazed-composition eye with a flat undetailed underside. TIP. c) Blue-green and black glazed-composition, double sided eye, filled with two rows of profile monkeys seated head on paws above a basket. TIP. d) Leaf-green glazed-composition eye. The convex upper side has a quadruple *wedjat* with rosette and lotus heads between. The flat underside has an incised *wedjat*. TIP. e) Yellow glazed-composition eye, plain backed. W. 3.5 cm, TIP. f) Two-tone glazed-composition, openwork eye in a frame. Double sided. TIP. g) Feldspar eye, convex on both faces. TIP. h) Two-tone glazed-composition eye with a highly convex top surface. Double sided. TIP. i) Red jasper, flat-backed, openwork eye with incised details. There is an upreared cobra wearing a disc at the front. 18th Dynasty. j) Two-tone glazed-composition, openwork, double sided eye. *Wedjats* and profile monkeys seated with head on paws appear in the interstices. TIP.

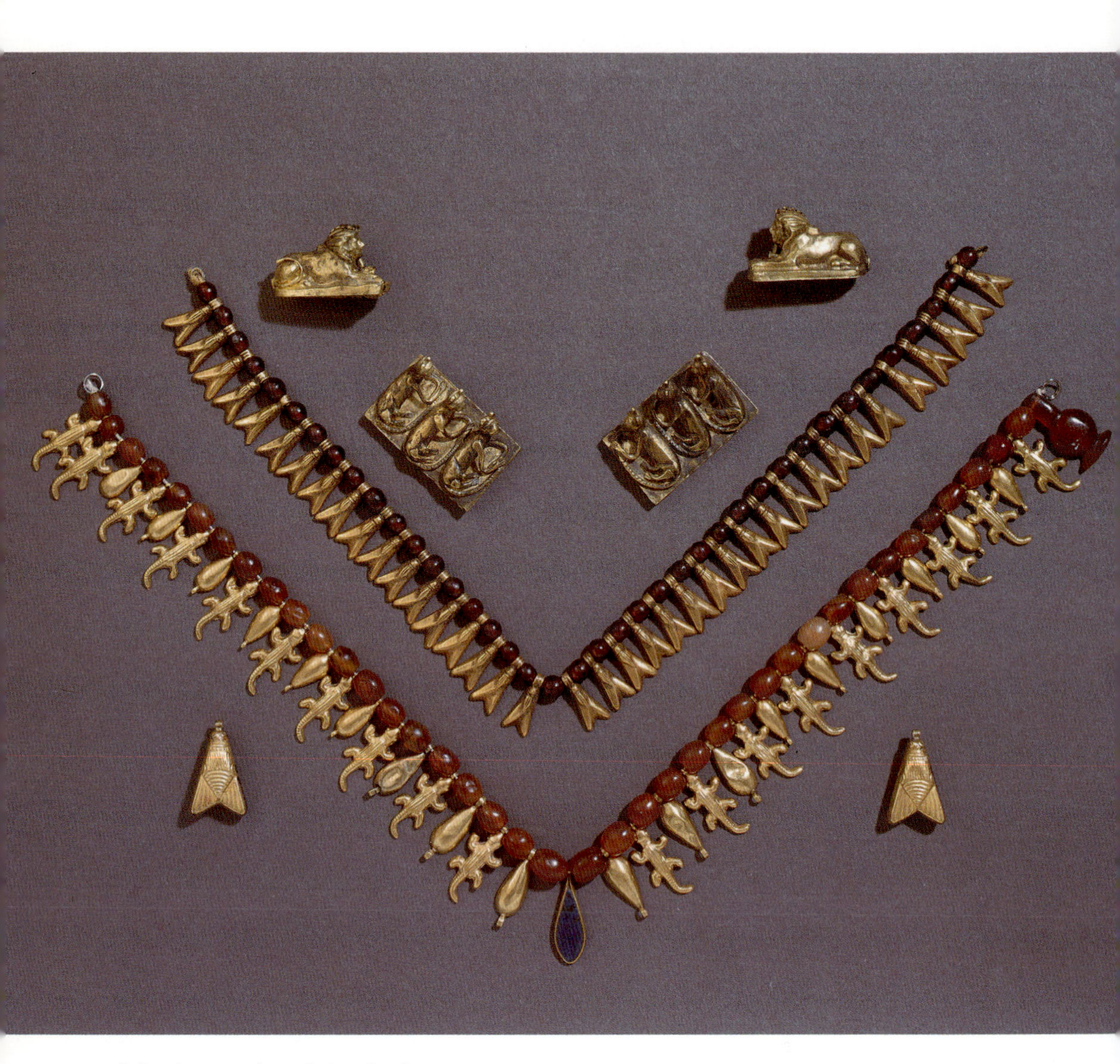

48 *Precious metal amuletic animals.*
FROM TOP TO BOTTOM a) Hollow gold pair of sphinx beads symbolising royal power. MK. b) Gold pair of spacer bars from a bracelet, each surmounted by three reclining cats. The underside names Queen Sobkemsaf, wife of King Nubkheperre Inyotef. L. 3 cm, 17th Dynasty (*c.*1650 BC). c) Solid-cast gold flies and garnet beads. 18th Dynasty. d) Hollow gold lizards, symbolic of regeneration, with gold date-shaped pendants, an inlaid gold drop and cornelian beads. 18th Dynasty. e) Pair of flies, an honorific award, in gold over core. NK.

cover c lazuli, jasper, breccia, serpentine, rock crystal, granite, amethyst, cornelian, glass and bronze 66i also occur. A distinctive glass type is characteristic of the Eighteenth Dynasty (see page 101). The burial of the wives of Tuthmosis III contained a number of hollow gold Thoeris pendants made by beating into a mould and soldering on a back-plate; seven others came from the Gold Tomb in the Valley of the Kings; and a number of further examples, just 43e as fine, are of unknown provenance. Unusual forms of Thoeris-Ipet include ones of 31b, c cornelian and feldspar with a cat's head, glazed-composition examples with female head in tripartite wig, and a curious green-glazed steatite type with detailed patterning rep- 39c, d resenting two figures back to back in profile of New Kingdom date.

The pendant amulet called *nḫȝw*, (*nekhau*), in the shape of a fish with a loop at its nose, was attached to the end of the plait of a child or young female as a charm against drowning. Presumably its magic worked by aversion: it was a reminder of the watery environment the wearer wished to avoid. Its first mention is in the literary text known as the Westcar Papyrus which dates to the Middle Kingdom, the time of the amulet's greatest popularity. Contemporary representations show it worn by a servant girl forming a support to a cosmetic container and by a tomb owner's daughter at Meir. Examples representing the *batensoda* fish modelled in the round are of hollow gold, silver 69a and electrum, sometimes with inlays. A second type, however, was flat with a green-stone inlay in a cloison as its body with added metal tail and fins, representing the *Tilapia* or *bolti* 43a, c fish which usually symbolised regeneration. It was certainly this form of the amulet which was lost by one of King Sneferu's harim girls as she rowed him on the lake, for in the Westcar text she refers to her '*nekau* of fresh turquoise'.

Amulets in the shape of various types of fish 4j pierced from end to end like a bead and made from glazed composition or semi-precious stones occur as early as the Sixth Dynasty; the burial of the wives of Tuthmosis III contained sufficient gold ones to form a triple-stringed girdle. Some of these amuletic beads might represent sacred fish: glazed steatite and silver examples of the *Barbus* are the *Lepidotus* of 93d classical sources, sacred to the lion goddess Mehyt. Those shaped like the *Tilapia* were 93c, 4j presumably worn for their symbolism of regeneration, but others must have embodied the idea of preservation from drowning by aversion like the *nekhau*.

Inanimate Forms

An *aegis* represents a deep broad bead collar surmounted by the head of a deity; its protective qualities are witnessed by the fact that one was set at the prow and stern of every temple god's sacred barque, the head being that of the god or goddess in question. Amulets in the form of an *aegis*, however, are connected with only a handful of deities: Bastet or possibly Tefnut as lion, Mut the Theban vulture goddess, Hathor, Amen-Re as ram and Bes. The head is usually frontal, though profile examples are known; suspension is always by means of a ring or tube behind the collar. All the goddesses wear the long tripartite wig; Bastet or Tefnut is crowned by the sun-disc with uraeus, human-headed Mut wears the Double Crown and Hathor the cow's horns and disc. Blue- or green-glazed composition, often with added colour, and cast bronze are the usual materials, but there are also some superb sheet-silver examples made by beating into a mould. The *aegis* as amulet first appears in the New Kingdom, but it is particularly common in the Third Intermediate Period and later. A type of finger-ring characteristic of the Third Intermediate Period, made from blue-green-glazed 45b, c composition, has a bezel in the form of a modelled *aegis* which sits at right angles to the shank. Often, though, close examination shows that the shank is actually formed by the pendulum-shaped body of a counterpoise for which the *aegis* serves as the topmost element.

The *menyet* was a form of collar particularly associated with the goddess Hathor. It was composed of multiple bead strings which required, as did all heavy collars, that a **counterpoise** be worn between the shoulder blades to counterbalance its weight and help it lie correctly over the chest. The counterpoise to the *menyet* collar was always pendulum-shaped and began to appear as an amulet at 97g least as early as the Ramesside Period, continuing until the end of the Ptolemaic Period.

Almost invariably the material is green- or blue-glazed composition, with a few examples of feldspar and later of bronze. Some are undecorated, but others, especially during the Third Intermediate Period, are increasingly ornate. A particularly popular form depicts at [40a, c, d] the top a lion goddess's head, either frontal or in profile, wearing a sun-disc or a human goddess's head set atop a large broad collar, the whole forming the independent amulet called an *aegis*. Upreared cobras frequently flank the central section of the amulet, which often contains a figured scene, especially one involving a lion goddess. The roundel at the base might be decorated with such motifs as a many-petalled flower, a *wedjat*-eye, a celestial barque, a floral knot or a scene with a child god on a lotus. Such highly ornate counterpoise amulets are manufactured in raised relief, differently coloured glazes or even openwork. The undecorated forms have a suspension tube along the flat top, the ornate examples have one behind the *aegis* head. All the goddesses represented on the counterpoise – Bastet, Tefnut, Mut and Hathor – had connotations of fertility but in addition were powerful deities who could afford protection. Moreover, the position of the counterpoise between the shoulder blades meant that it could guard this most vulnerable area. The protective function of this amulet is surely proved by the rare examples in which [40d] the *aegis* is topped by the heads of Tefnut and her consort Shu wearing tall feathers: in identical full-sized bronze counterpoises the inscription states that they are providing '*sa*' – a magical protection.

Also connected with the protection of women and children are amuletic **cylindrical** [42] **pendants**, which are particularly characteristic of the Middle Kingdom, although they continued in use until after the New Kingdom. They exist in two forms. One type is of gold, silver or electrum with a hollow shaft, often decorated with granulation or rope braid patterning, and a removable conical cap at each end, the upper with a suspension loop so that the article might be worn about the neck. Mereret's treasure at Dahshur contained one of gold; three of gold and another of silver came from the burial of the wives of Tuthmosis III. Other fine non-royal examples are of Middle Kingdom date. Although some later cylinders still held a rolled-up papyrus with a text for the protection of mothers and children, many earlier ones contain only one or more garnets of unknown symbolism. The second type of cylindrical pendant is solid with a shaft of gold or silver bands alternating with short cylinder beads of amethyst, feldspar, lapis lazuli, cornelian, turquoise or even rock crystal, all on a rod. Both Sithathor and Mereret at Dahshur owned one and there are a number of examples from non-royal burials of contemporary date. Thus the hollow cylinders were amulet cases and the solid ones dummies in the same shape.

The **cowrie shell** was believed to have [49c, g] amuletic significance because of its resemblance to the female genitalia, so when beads in [64k] its shape formed an element of a woman's girdle they were in exactly the right place to ward off evil influences from the relevant bodily part of the wearer, especially if she were pregnant. Although actual shells must have served this purpose in predynastic burials, as early as the Sixth Dynasty they were being imitated in blue-glazed composition and shortly thereafter in cornelian and quartz. During the First Intermediate Period bone buckle-beads served as a cheaper imitation. A [74g] considerable number of hollow gold, silver and electrum cowries made in two halves punched [69a] into a mould and soldered around the outer edge, have survived from Middle Kingdom burials. Those serving as clasps have base plate soldered to each half bearing a tongue-and-groove closing device. Hollow gold cowries in the girdles owned by Sithathoriunet and Mereret contained metal pellets which would have made a tinkling sound as they walked. From the Middle Kingdom onwards a type of amulet in which the scarab-form back is replaced by that of a stylised cowrie is termed a cowroid. [55d, e]

In the New Kingdom a semi-circular amuletic bead also based on a stylised cowrie, called a **wallet bead**, because the markings around the [43b] curved edge resemble stitching, ousted the shell from girdles. Not only hollow silver and gold examples but ones made from lapis lazuli, green-glazed steatite, red jasper and blue-glazed composition have been found in both royal and private burials until as late as the Twenty-second Dynasty. Another feature of womens' girdles during the Middle and New

Kingdoms are lenticular beads with a spouted stringing hole resembling acacia seeds; these are made from lapis lazuli, cornelian, turquoise feldspar, glass and hollow gold. In the New Kingdom only, ribbed flattened ball beads of lapis lazuli, feldspar and hollow gold occur, apparently imitating nasturtium seeds. Both forms must be amuletic but their symbolism is unclear.

The **oyster-shell** amulet, called in Egyptian *wḏ3* (*wedja*), meaning 'sound, whole, healthy', naturally enough was thought to endow its wearer with these attributes. It seems to have been another women's ornament, for examples have been found among the treasures of Mereret, Sithathor, Khnumet, Senebtisy and Nubhotepti, and it is most often depicted worn at a woman's neck. It was particularly popular during the Middle Kingdom, although one of gold and another of silver were found in the burial of the wives of Tuthmosis III. Usually 43d plain sheet gold, silver or electrum was beaten into a mould, but some particularly fine examples, like those of Mereret, were further inlaid with semi-precious stones; others have a repoussé decoration. A burial at Haraga contained fourteen natural shells set in silver. Other shell-shaped amulets, mostly in semi-precious stones and almost all of Middle Kingdom date, though again examples come from the burial of the wives of Tuthmosis III, imitate in particular ***conus***. Those in the shape of ***nerita*** first appear in Sixth Dynasty burials, 5j others resembling ***cardium edule*** even earlier in the late Predynastic Period; twenty-four gold mollusc shells were found in a First Dynasty tomb at Nag ed-Deir. All must have served an amuletic purpose, as did the real shells they imitate.

Curiously enough, amulets in the shape of the hieroglyph meaning 'protection' – *s3* (*sa*) – are very rare and virtually confined to the Middle Kingdom, although as a protective motif the form first occurs in the early Old Kingdom and continued to be prominent throughout the Dynastic Period. The ***sa*** represents a rolled-up reed mat folded in two and tied near the lower end; it was carried as portable furniture by marsh dwellers and cattle herders who also pressed it into service as a lifejacket and a guard over sharp horns. Most of the examples to survive are of gold, silver, electrum or copper wires imitating the reed 49d stalks and their binding, although Senebtisy 64p also owned a number made from cornelian, feldspar and ivory. At Dahshur, Khnumet's burial contained two superb bracelet clasps, each formed from an openwork gold *sa* in a frame, the top surface inlaid with lapis lazuli except for the ties which are of cornelian and turquoise; the same details are incised on the gold of the underside. At the top of each amulet is a tiny gold leopard's (or lioness's) head.

Without doubt the best-known of all protective amulets is the ***wḏ3.t*** (***wedjat*** or ***udjat* eye**), literally 'the sound one', referring to the eye of the falcon-headed Horus after it had been plucked out during one of his interminable battles with Seth and then healed by Thoth. This Horus was the elder (Greek Haroeris), the celestial falcon and great creator god whose right eye was the sun and left eye the moon. It is generally supposed that the *wedjat* was the moon eye, which was 'injured' as it waned and 'restored' as it waxed each month, but the term might just as well apply to the sun eye, the 'sound' one as opposed to the 'injured' one. When Osiris rose to pre-eminence as the god of the dead, the *wedjat* became identified with the eye of his son Horus. According to the Osiris myth, Horus offered the healed eye to his dead father and so powerful a charm was it that it restored him to life. The offering of the *wedjat* would even suffice instead of actual food offerings in the daily ritual. Its great protective qualities can be seen from the fact it was often depicted on the plate which covered the embalming incision in the mummy's flank. Not only would it prevent malign influences entering, but it would also magically heal the wound. The *wedjat* is probably found in greater numbers on mummies than any other amulet, 7c, d but, of course, it could also be worn in life.

At its most basic the *wedjat* is a human eye with brow above and markings below; the latter take the form of a drop shape at the front and an uncurling spiral at the back, said to imitate the markings on the head of the lanner falcon. Curiously enough, both right and left eye can be represented. The *wedjat* amulet is first found in the later Old Kingdom and it contin- 4i ued to be produced until the Roman Period, though, as might be expected over so long a time, its forms are many and varied. Even the materials from which it was made are as different as glazed composition and glass, both plain and polychrome, feldspar, lapis lazuli, amethyst, sard, cornelian, chalcedony, obsidian, porphyry, haematite, agate, diorite, steatite, serpentine and gold.

The earliest *wedjats* are mostly very stylised, and formed from chunky cornelian or roughly moulded glazed composition, although by the First Intermediate Period delicate openwork sheet gold examples were already being made. Elaborate glazed-composition *wedjats*, openwork or inlaid, with a crowned uraeus hanging from the front edge of the brow, or those in which the drop is turned into a falcon's leg or a human arm grasping an *ankh*, *nefer* sign or ostrich feather and the rear spiral is transmogrified into bird's tail feathers, first occur in the New Kingdom. The most ornate forms, however, date to the Third Intermediate Period and Twenty-fifth Dynasty. Some have a Bes head, ibis, walking bull or rosette in the space above the spiral; others are surmounted by a frieze of uraei or even have a lioness reclining along the top of the brow. In splendid openwork examples tiny *wedjats* turned in every direction or rows of uraei, seated cats or even monkeys, are inserted into every available space. Yet other contemporary pieces are *wedjats* in outline only, with a mere blob of different-coloured glaze for the pupil and a stripe for the brow, or else they are large, clumsily shaped and very thick with a domed upper surface. Glazed-composition plaques with a high-relief *wedjat* on one face set in an ornately decorated background, openwork *wedjats* in a rosette and pylon-shaped pectorals adorned with *wedjats* first appear in the Third Intermediate Period but continue into the Late Period. Openwork *wedjats* as the bezel of all-in-one glazed-composition finger-rings and scaraboids with their backs carved in the shape of a *wedjat* are typical of the Nineteenth Dynasty; openwork barrel beads with a pattern of *wedjats* are characteristic of the Third Intermediate Period.

If one *wedjat* gave protection, multiple *wedjats* would furnish even more: during the Third Intermediate Period some forms of the amulet, both openwork and solid, comprise four *wedjats* (two on top of two). Sometimes only the lower two have the characteristic markings below, sometimes all have them, with the top two turned upside down to accommodate them; any available space is filled with elaborate patterning. Yet while all these highly decorated types of *wedjats* were being produced, the basic form continued to be made, frequently in fine, hard, sharply detailed monochrome-glazed composition or even with polychrome glaze inlays. For all forms of *wedjat*, suspension was by a hole through the length or a loop at the top.

Particularly symbolic of protection yet extremely rare as an amulet and unique to the Ptolemaic Period is the **Winged Sun disc**. It represents the sun god flanked by the protective wings of the falcon god Horus of Edfu and is a motif carved above every doorway in every Late Period temple. Amuletic examples exist in steatite, silver and glass.

The figure-of-eight **knot**, *ṯs* (*tjes*), made in two parts from hollow gold shaped in a mould and with a tongue-and-groove closing device on the two flat undersides, was a characteristic element of Middle Kingdom jewellery. The burials of Khnumet, Sithathor, Sithathoriunet, Mereret and Senebtisy all contained a number which served as clasps for anklets and bracelets. However, examples of solid lapis lazuli, cornelian, amethyst and chrysoprase, which are probably contemporary, show that the *tjes* also existed as an amulet, presumably with the funerary connotation of protection by binding or union, for the Egyptians had a horror that their limbs, head and torso might become separated in the Other World. A form of **scaraboid** found in the New Kingdom with a back resembling a large, tightened bow but actually made from two flower-heads joined or possibly a bundle of grain, may well represent a later development of the knot.

Osirian Protection

A funerary amulet closely connected with the Osiris legend is the ***tit*** or **Girdle of Isis** prescribed by Chapter 156 of the *Book of the Dead* and to be made of red jasper, the colour of the blood of the goddess. If one was placed on the neck of the mummy, 'the power of Isis will be the protection of his body'. The standard form of this amulet is an open loop of material from whose bound lower end hangs a long sash flan-

49 *Protective amulets.*
From LEFT to RIGHT a) Sheet silver incised winged sun disc with flanking uraei. W. 8 cm, LD. b) Hollow sheet-gold knot clasp made in two halves showing the tongue-and-groove closing device on the underside. MK. c) Grey-green glazed-composition cowrie underside showing a faithful reproduction of shell. The top shows a seated cat with an ostrich feather. NK to TIP. d) Electrum wire *sa* amulet. MK. e) Red jasper *tit* amulet inscribed for the priest of Ptah and Thoth Iryiry. H. 7 cm, NK. f) Turquoise-blue glazed-composition *tit* amulet with back-pillar. Saite. g) Leaf green glazed-composition openwork cowrie with a lunar seated baboon facing a winged uraeus wearing a disc. NK to TIP.

ked by two folded loops, perhaps representing a cloth worn during menstruation. Although many *tit*-amulets are indeed of prescribed red jasper, glass or cornelian, many are also of green-glazed composition or glass, another regenerative colour. They first make an appearance at about the same time they are first depicted in funerary papyrus vignettes. One of the earliest has been identified on the mummy of Kha, Chief workman at Deir el-Medina under King Amenophis III; another came from the burial of Akhenaten's vizier, Aper-el, at Saqqara. Akhenaten's grandfather Yuya was buried with one of red glass. Thereafter, until the end of dynastic history, no mummy was knowingly interred without one among its wrappings, almost invariably over the upper torso.

64q, 7h, 49f

3, 100a

63

89a

When the stomach, lungs, liver and intestines were removed from the corpse during the embalming process, they were dried out in natron, anointed with unguents, coated with resin and wrapped in linen before being placed in four containers called Canopic Jars. By the end of the Eighteenth Dynasty the stoppers of the jars were shaped into the heads of the **Canopic Deities**, the **Four Sons of Horus**. Falcon-headed Qebhsenuef guarded the intestines, human-form Imsety the liver, baboon-headed Hapy protected the lungs and jackal-headed Duamutef the stomach. During the Third Intermediate Period, however, mummification practices changed and the packages containing the embalmed internal organs were no longer placed in Canopic Jars but were returned to the body cavity, each with an amuletic figure of the relevant deity attached. Made almost exclusively of glazed composition or glass, often multicoloured (though sometimes pottery or wax was used and even more rarely sheet gold or silver), the four are always represented full length and wrapped like a mummy either in profile or frontal with flat back. Usually the arms are not shown, but sometimes the hands emerge clasping a folded cloth. Although later canopic packages came to be placed once more inside jars or within the mummy wrappings, an amuletic set of the Four Sons of Horus contin-

16c

50, 51

50 and **51** *Sons of Horus.* LEFT Turquoise-blue glazed-composition flat-backed set of the Four Sons of Horus in profile each holding a long folded cloth. Imsety and Duamutef face right, Qebhsenuef and Hapy face left. 25th Dynasty or later.
BELOW LEFT a) Pale turquoise-blue glazed-composition baboon-headed Hapy, in the round, against a plaque and holding a folded cloth in each hand. Saite. b) Turquoise-blue glazed-composition falcon-headed Qebhsenuef in the round holding a folded cloth. Saite. c) Blue-green glazed-composition plaque incised with a human-headed Imsety, in profile, holding the symbol of the West. LP. d) Black glass flat-backed jackal-headed Duamutef, in profile. H. 6.9 cm, Ptolemaic.

ued to be supplied, usually stitched on to the bandages over the torso by means of the holes provided in the figures or incorporated into the bead netting which enveloped contemporary mummies.

7g

Jackal-form **Anubis** as an amulet would have been worn only by the dead. Like the crocodile, the black jackal was a dangerous force to be propitiated. Since its chief activity was prowling around desert cemeteries seeking bones to crunch or skulking around embalmers' storage rooms in the hope of carrying off a well-salted limb from an unsupervised corpse as it lay drying out in natron, and destruction of the body prevented an Afterlife, Anubis was deified as god of embalming, doomed to protect the very object he would by nature attack. According to legend he was the son of Osiris and Nephthys and practised his embalming skills for the very first time on his father's corpse.

13c

The earliest jackal-form amulet, made of bone, was found in a predynastic Naqada 2 burial and shows the animal couchant, in profile and with the scored markings characteristic of contemporary amulets. By the Sixth Dynasty glazed-composition walking jackals and, rather more significantly, jackal-headed walking human figures occur, the earliest amuletic representation of an animal-headed deity. Perhaps the chief embalmer already donned a jackal's mask to carry out his work and this is how the iconography came to be established. The jackal standing with back legs at a slope or couchant with dangling tail on top of a pylon-shaped chest was being made by the Middle Kingdom: examples of both types in gold were found in a Twelfth Dynasty burial at Abydos.

38i

Thereafter these two forms and the jackal-headed deity, both walking and seated, continued to be made until the end of dynastic history, generally in glazed composition or metal. The question arises, however, whether the animal depicted is always a jackal. Certainly the one on the shrine represents Anubis as lord of the funerary chest and guardian of the necropolis and is often shown thus on funerary pectorals. The animal-headed deity is almost certainly Anubis, but the animal with characteristically sloping back legs may rather represent the wolf god **Wepwawet** of Asyut, the 'Opener-of-the-Ways', who adopts this posture on standards carried before the king in processions. Without any indication of colouring – Wepwawet was grey – identification cannot be definite. Particularly fine examples of this type come from the burial of the Meroitic Queen Amanishakheto at Meroe. Four are in pairs and in two of them the tall-eared long-tailed creature's head is supported by a uraeus, a feature repeated in glazed-composition pieces.

An unusual Late Period amulet in finely modelled glazed composition representing a jackal-headed man wearing a sun-disc, seated on a throne and drawing a bow with arrow, may actually be a variant **hybrid figure** (see page 37), for at the back his body is transformed into a bird's complete with long tail feathers.

Amulets of **Osiris**, god of the dead *par excellence*, are surprisingly rare. Apart from an inlaid gold example standing in profile and two tiny, finely detailed, solid-cast seated and squatting ones from the Twenty-second Dynasty burial of Prince Hornakht at Tanis and an unprovenanced standing silver piece which may be contemporary, only a few of glazed composition and glass, some three-dimensional, others in profile, and some small solid-cast bronzes, all of Late Period date, are known. One unusual example depicts five thin bronze Osiris figures all in a row. It is noteworthy that many small bronzes of the god not only have suspension loops but also a tang beneath the feet and so, though light enough, were not intended to be worn. Characteristically the god is completely human, wrapped like a mummy, wears the royal beard and White Crown or *atef*-crown and carries the crook and flail, all attributes he subsumed very early on from Andjety, a local deified dead king of Busiris, for originally Osiris was the formless

52 *Unusual animal-headed gods.*
a) Seated jackal-headed archer, with bird's wings and tail, wearing a disc, probably representing a divine protective power. Pale green glazed composition. LP.
b) Boar-headed man, probably representing a form of the sun-god, in pale green glazed composition. H. 8.3 cm, TIP.

fertile black Egyptian earth.

Often, of course, Osiris is the chief figure in funerary jewellery. A unique pendant inscribed with the name of Osorkon II and possibly from his burial at Tanis shows the god in cast gold squatting on a tall block of lapis lazuli capped with a gold cavetto cornice. He is flanked by two superbly modelled solid-gold figures, standing on an inlaid-gold plinth, of his falcon-headed son Horus wearing the Double Crown and his sister-wife Isis in horns and disc, each with an arm upraised in protection. A suspension loop is behind each figure. The same three deities squatting one behind the other in relief are also the subject of Late Dynastic glazed-composition pectoral amulets. A more usual pylon-shaped pectoral from Tutankhamun's burial, made from inlaid openwork gold, depicts the vulture Nekhbet wearing the *atef*-crown and the winged cobra Wadjyt in the Red Crown, both on inlaid baskets, opening their wings about a standing mummiform Osiris who is crowned with the *atef* and holds the flail and a crook with an abnormally long stock. The inscriptions show that the protective goddesses of Upper and Lower Egypt had become totally assimilated with Isis and Nephthys. Far more unusual is the pylon-shaped pectoral from the burial of Amenemope at Tanis made from two sheets of gold with a thin filling between, for one face bears a scene in repoussé, the other the same scene incised. In both Amenemope is depicted raising an incense burner to the enthroned god. Osiris also usually appears on one side of solid pylon-shaped funerary pectorals made from polychrome-glazed composition and on one type of heart scarab (see page 57).

Of the main protagonists in the Osiris legend, some occur in an amuletic form which is clearly intended to afford particular funerary protection. 66d, 53b **Isis and Nephthys mourning**, usually as a matched pair, kneeling or standing with hand to the head in characteristic gesture of lamentation, made in an open-backed mould from glass or glazed composition, are particularly Ptolemaic in date. Placed on the upper chest of a mummy, they would afford it the same protection that they gave to the corpse of their brother Osiris.

Although one of the four protectresses of the dead, **Nephthys** (in Egyptian, *Nbt-ḥwt*) most often appears in amuletic form as a member of the family of Osiris, sister and helper of Isis and Osiris (to whom she bore Anubis), and wife of Seth. Amulets representing her as a woman wearing on her head the two hieroglyphic components of her name occur later in burials than those of other players in the drama. Although a single seated gold example came from the Twenty-second Dynasty burial of Hornakht at Tanis and an identical silver piece may be of similar date, no others are recorded before the Twenty-sixty Dynasty. Thereafter, however, in glazed composition and lapis lazuli, her standing figure is found on every mummy, usually on the upper torso in the company of amulets of Isis. Even the Buchis-bull mummies were buried with them in their wrappings.

Amulets of **Isis**, however, appeared earlier, for she was primarily the archetypal protective mother goddess. Although in the Late Period amulets in glazed composition, lapis lazuli and even gold are found on every mummy, usually on the chest, representing her merely standing with the hieroglyph for 'throne' which writes her name upon her head, her most characteristic guise is as a seated, suckling mother with the infant Horus propped up by her left hand. 18b Such an amulet is actually specified in the MacGregor Papyrus list. Small glazed amulets in this shape are already found in the Ramesside Period, but they are more numerous in burials of the Third Intermediate Period and later. Often details are picked out in a darker-coloured glaze and the throne on which Isis sits is openwork, the sides adorned with the sinuous body of the snake god Nehebkau. Later, cast bronze and flat-backed mould-made glass examples occur too. However, just as often as figures of this goddess wear the hieroglyph for her name on their heads, they wear the horns and disc, leading to confusion with Hathor. 18a Indeed one of the finest and largest solid-gold amulets from the burial of Wendjebauendjed at Tanis, still on its loop-in-loop chain, depicts a superbly modelled, standing female figure wearing the horns and disc but specifically named on the base as 'Isis, the divine mother'.

Of course, amulets of Isis with Horus could protect women and children just as well in this world as in the next. The goddess's guardian function is especially seen in an unusual 17b glazed-composition example in which her

53 *Unusual forms of Osirian myth participants.*
a) Green and yellow glazed-composition Anubis in centurian costume with a spear. Roman. b) Blue-green glazed-composition flat-backed plaque incised with Nephthys in the mourning posture. H 5.6 cm, G-R. c) Flat-backed seated Osiris in profile, wearing the *atef*-crown and carrying a crook and flail. Blue-green glazed composition. LP. d) Plaque showing Isis, Horus and Nephthys in relief profile. Turquoise-blue glazed composition. W. 2 cm, LP.

standing figure wearing horns and disc and carrying a papyrus sceptre is enveloped by the winged arms of a double of herself standing behind.

A characteristic amulet of the Saite Period, usually made from sharply detailed glazed composition but in cast bronze too, takes the form of a plaque from which emerge in high back cover b relief the frontal figures of the **Osirian triad**: Isis and Nephthys flanking and holding the hands of Horus-the-Child, who is naked and wears the side-lock. The order of the goddesses 53d is sometimes reversed and the figures can be in profile. This amulet is most often found on the lower torso, sometimes more than one example on a single mummy.

Amulets of **Thoth** as a walking ibis-headed 38h man carrying the *wedjat*-eye before him relate directly to the power of the eye of Horus to revive the dead Osiris and thus any of the dead, and to provide food offerings in the Other World. Glazed-composition examples in the round first appear in non-royal burials of Third Intermediate Period date, although superbly modelled ones are characteristically Saite. Sometimes the *wedjat* is turned sideways to support the long beak, a technical feature unnecessary in tiny, finely detailed, solid-cast gold examples from the Tanis royal burials and in other unprovenanced precious metal pieces, possibly of a similar date. However, even without the *wedjat*, ibis-headed Thoth as amulet had a purely funerary connotation: a squatting example made of gold inlaid with feldspar was found around the neck of Tutankhamun's mummy, and standing examples were always 7e, 20a, frontis placed on the chests of Late Period mummies in a row with the other funerary deities.

Ibis-form amulets first found in burials of First Intermediate Period date, invariably of gold, electrum or copper, usually perch on a 62a standard, suggesting that the god must be intended. By the Third Intermediate Period at least, the long beak of well-made metal examples, whether standing or crouched, is often supported by an ostrich feather and this, 21f or the squatting figure of Maat herself, was usually the supporting element in ibis amulets of glazed composition, sometimes two-toned, lapis lazuli, olivine and glass until the end of the dynastic period. This gives the ibis amulet too a purely funerary connotation, for the presence of Maat or her symbol is a visual reminder of Thoth's role as recorder of the result of the weighing of the deceased's heart in the Underworld. The occasional substitution of an obelisk for beak support is a play on the word *tekhen* which means 'ibis', 'obelisk' and 'Eye of Horus'; the substitution of a baboon is a reference to Thoth's other animal manifestation.

4

Scarabs for the Living and Funerary Scarabs

The amulet in the form of a scarab is perhaps the best known of all those manufactured by the ancient Egyptians; it was certainly the most numerous. Hundreds of thousands of scarabs were made in ancient times over a period of some two thousand years from the First Intermediate Period until the Graeco-Roman Period and not just in Egypt, for the form was soon copied by local craftsmen in Syria and Palestine. Virtually every material known to the Egyptians was used in their manufacture, from precious metal, semi-precious and non-precious stones to glazed composition and glass. Indeed three of the earliest known firmly dated small glass objects of native Egyptian manufacture are scarabs bearing the names of Twelfth Dynasty officials. However, from their earliest appearance the commonest material was glazed steatite; only in the New Kingdom did glazed composition rival it. Of the others, amethyst, rock crystal, feldspar and green jasper are characteristic for pre-New Kingdom scarabs; thereafter red jasper, cornelian and lapis lazuli are more popular. Except for funerary and royal commemorative examples, scarabs are noteworthy for their generally small size (0.5 to 2.5cm is the normal range in length) and the remarkable sharpness of the texts and figures on the best of them. But why should this form of amulet have become so popular?

The characteristic behaviour of the Egyptian scarab (*Scarabaeus sacer*) or dung beetle which is most commonly found in the Western Desert is to roll a large ball of animal dung with its back legs to an underground hiding place where it serves as a foodstuff. Such is the size of the ball that the beetle has to stand almost on its head while pushing and usually has to do so for a considerable distance. Since the scarab is unable to see where it is going, it often takes a route which is not only circuitous but beset

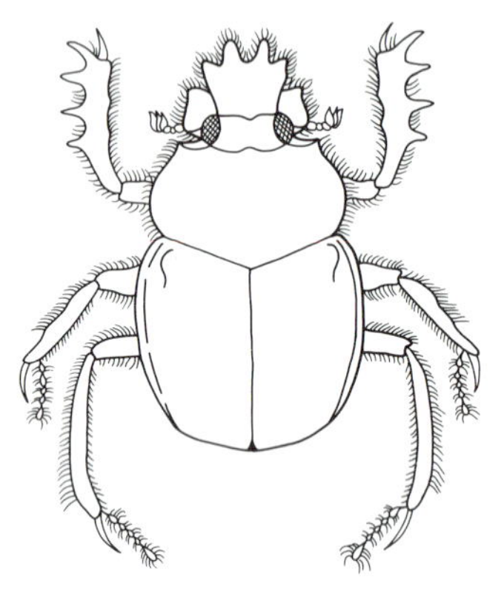

with obstacles. Occasionally it will even attempt to roll the ball of dung up an almost vertical surface and will not give up until virtually exhausted. Such persistent toil did not go unnoticed by the ancient Egyptians, who very quickly likened the rolling of the ball of dung to the passage of the sun-disc across the heavens each day from east to west, pushed by a gigantic black beetle of course!

In addition scarab eggs are laid in a ball of dung which feeds the larvae it contains and is also stored underground. It is created there by the female exclusively from sheep excrement and is pear-shaped, not round. Nevertheless, it is understandable that the Egyptians were led to believe that the baby beetles hatched from one and the same type of dung ball. Thus the scarab became a symbol of spontaneous generation, new life and, by extension, resurrection. Indeed, this linking of the scarab with death and the ability to transcend it can only have been enhanced by the behaviour of mature beetles, which sometimes appear to burst out of the earth from their empty underground larders when a new and smelly heap of dung has been deposited in the vicinity. It may not have gone unnoticed either that the appearance of the pupa, whose wings and legs are encased at that stage of development, is very mummy-like. It has even been pointed out that the egg-bearing ball of dung is created in an underground chamber which is reached by a vertical shaft and horizontal passage curiously reminiscent of the internal plan of Old Kingdom mastaba tombs. Did Egyptian funerary architecture deliberately imitate the scarab's breeding place in a conscious attempt to provide the dead with the same possibility of new life?

All the misapprehensions about the habits of the scarab were also recorded by classical authors such as Plutarch and Horapollo with additional embellishments such as the belief that all scarabs are male – since copulation takes place underground it is rarely witnessed – and that the hatching-out period from the eggs is twenty-nine days, the latter to provide some kind of link with the lunar cycle. However, Horapollo's report that the egg-bearing ball had to be thrown into the Nile so that the new-born beetle could emerge does have a kernel of truth to it. If the ball dries out, moisture is necessary to release the new scarab and the inundation would certainly provide it.

As a hieroglyph the scarab has the phonetic value *ḫpr* (*kheper*) which as a verb means 'to come into being', 'to be created', and as a noun 'form' or 'manifestation'. According to the legend of creation centred on the city of Heliopolis, in which the sun god had three different manifestations depending on the time of day, the new-born sun was called Khepri and usually took the form of a man with a scarab beetle for a head. Unlike other hybrid deities, who were given an animal's head instead of a human one, Khepri had to have a whole scarab perched on his shoulders – a beetle's head would have been too tiny and indistinguishable for the purpose.

However, it was always as a large black beetle that Khepri was depicted in funerary scenes representing the passage of the sun god from night and darkness into the new day and new life. The funerary text known as the *Imy Duat* (the *Book of the One who is in the Underworld*) is found essentially on the walls of royal tombs of New Kingdom date in the Valley of the Kings and also on non-royal funerary papyri of the succeeding Third Intermediate Period. There at the end of the twelfth hour of night the sun god takes the form of a scarab to emerge into the day on the arms of the air god Shu. Similarly in the last scene of another funerary composition known as the *Book of Caverns*, as the sun breaks through the boundary of the Underworld, one of the shapes he assumes is that of a scarab. In the final part of the *Book of the Night* too, where the goddess Nut, whose arched body forms the vault of heaven, gives birth to her sun child, he is in scarab form. Even in the final scene of the *Book of Gates*, in which the whole of the cycle of creation is represented pictorially, it is a scarab in the solar barque which raises up the sun-disc into the waiting arms of the Underworld sky goddess. Sometimes in these examples the scarab is winged, an acknowledgement that the dung beetle can indeed fly, but also an enhancement of the concept of the scarab rising up towards heaven in resurrection.

It is thus scarcely surprising that the scarab became the most popular of all amulets and amuletic motifs, especially for the dead but also in the world of the living. Because of the underlying ideas inherent in its shape the scarab form of itself offered the hope of new life and resurrection, but these magical properties could be enhanced even further by the inscription, motifs or pictorial representations added to the flat underside. Yet the scarab made a surprisingly late appearance among the repertoire of amuletic forms which, as has been seen, occur as early as the predynastic Badarian Period. It is not until the Sixth Dynasty some two thousand years later that the first scarabs are found, and their appearance is scarcely recognisable compared to their developed form. They are crudely shaped, almost exclusively from glazed steatite with some glazed composition, with legs splayed out at the sides and broad grooves on the back to indicate divisions between the wing-cases and prothorax. This

51

elementary type, which continued to be manufactured during the early First Intermediate Period, obviously functioned purely as an amulet, for the flat underside is undecorated. What distinguishes contemporary seal amulets is that, whether the base is circular, square or rectangular and the back shaped like a pyramid, a button shank (hence button seals) or even surmounted by couchant animals or squatting human figures, they all have a pattern or design carved on the underside which warrants their being termed a seal.

Scarabs and Scaraboids

By the mid-First Intermediate Period, however, many scarabs too were beginning to function as seals. Their back markings are still rudimentary, and though the legs are now bent at the sides of the body they are still not well delineated; nevertheless the underside bears the same maze-like patterns as contemporary seals. By the end of the period the repertoire of designs on scarabs had expanded to include geometrical patterns, often split into two mirror-image halves, stick-like humans, plants and animals. Even more important, the back of the scarab came to be carved to represent the insect naturalistically in the round with well-defined legs, its body raised from the plinth on

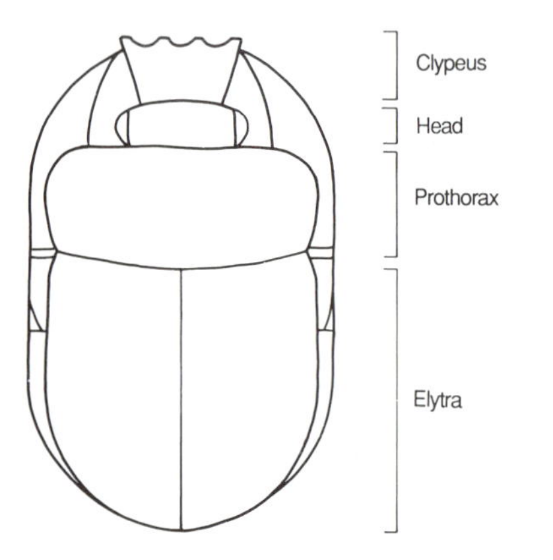

which it stands. Already in some examples all the characteristic features of the back of a 'developed' scarab amulet are present. The crinkly edged clypeus above the head is shown. A shallowly curving groove separates the broad prothorax from the long narrow wing-cases, which are themselves divided by one or more striations. The legs, too, are often realistically scored with markings called, rather confusingly, 'feathering'. Yet well into the New Kingdom it was obviously an arbitrary choice on the part of the craftsman as to which of these features or their variants were present and in which combination. All this without taking into consideration such subtle differences as the height of the insect's body above the plinth, whether the legs are represented extended or folded, the size, configuration and angle of the head and the profile of the back. Only the presence of a V-shaped notch at the top of each wing-case from the reign of Tuthmosis III onwards can be counted upon. Otherwise, virtually the only certainty about any scarab amulet is that its iconography is almost certainly not quite like that of any other!

In the Middle Kingdom the use of the scarab as a seal becomes firmly established. Not only have actual mud sealings with the impressions of scarabs' inscriptions survived, but a particularly numerous class of the object bears on the underside the titles and names of its owner which could have had little use except as a seal. Those with the names of kings, however, were probably worn as a sign of royal favour, for royalty of the period seems to have preferred to use magnificent cylinder-shaped seals. Until now, scarabs were worn either alone or with other amulets or beads, threaded on fibres or wires through the piercing which always runs from head to tail of the insect. During the Twelfth Dynasty scarabs form the bezels of finger-rings for the first time. At Lahun, Sithathoriunet owned two scarab finger-rings with the simplest of settings: in each the ends of the gold wire on which the inlaid gold scarab was threaded were twisted together opposite the amulet. Mereret's cache at Dahshur also contained gold rings with scarab bezels made from lapis lazuli, turquoise, amethyst and glazed composition, some with texts, the others uninscribed; the latter, of course, functioning purely as an amulet. Contemporary non-royal burials contained scarab finger-rings of a more elaborate form. The shanks are of tubular gold, their ends beaten out into wire which passed through the scarab bezel and was wound around the shank on both sides. The semi-precious stone scarabs are set in a gold funda or rimmed with gold so that the underside can be

45a, d

54 *Animal-backed scaraboids.*
From LEFT to RIGHT a) Green glazed steatite hedgehog. There are powerful hieroglyphic symbols on the underside. LP, imitation of SIP. b) Steatite frog with an elaborate rosette on the underside. SIP. c) Steatite plaque with a relief monkey and *nefer*-sign. The underside shows a horse and has the message 'Bastet gives vigilance'. Ramesside to TIP. d) Steatite duck with head bent back. The underside has the cartouche of Neferkare. L. 3.2 cm, 25th Dynasty (Shabaka, *c.* 710 BC). e) Steatite pair of crocodiles, snout to tail. The underside shows seated deities. SIP. f) Steatite kneeling antelope. There is a beast-tamer over a walking sphinx on the underside. NK to TIP. g) Pale turquoise-blue glazed-composition hedgehog. The underside has two crocodiles. NK. h) Dark green glazed steatite plaque with *Tilapia* in relief. The underside has a monkey and bears the message 'Bastet gives good'. Ramesside. i) Blue-green glazed steatite plaque with a lunar baboon in relief. The underside shows a lunar baboon and a human Khonsu. Ramesside. j) Blue-green glazed steatite reclining hippopotamus. Seth and Amun are on the underside. Ramesside. k) Blue-green glazed steatite reclining lion, one paw over the other. There is a lion on the underside. SIP.

seen. The latter was the method of mounting which became most popular for any swivelling bezel. It enabled a scarab to be worn back uppermost across the finger as an amulet, which could then be flipped over to reveal the underside for use as a seal or to display a scene or message. Although scarab finger-rings continued to be made until the end of pharaonic history, they soon lost their pre-eminence as seals to the solid-metal signet ring, which was far better able to withstand the pressure exerted during sealing. However, they continued to be worn as amuletic jewellery because of the potency of the scarab as an amulet in its own right and the possibility of enhancing its magical properties by the text or scene added to its underside.

Even before the end of the First Intermediate Period the underside of scarabs was decorated with living creatures symbolic of fecundity or regeneration such as the fly, fish, lizard, lion, cobra, crocodile, antelope and monkey, often represented in heraldic opposition; all of them continued as a decorative theme until at least the late New Kingdom. Sometimes, of course, instead of decorating the base these creatures, carved in high relief or even three-dimensionally, replaced the scarab back itself, this form of amulet being termed a **scaraboid**. Other popular shapes for scaraboid backs include cats, ducks, frogs, hippopotamuses, falcons, baboons, hedgehogs and even rams' heads. During the New Kingdom *wedjat*-eyes, Bes heads, Hathor heads and

54

55 *Decoratively-backed seals.* From LEFT to RIGHT
a) Steatite plaque with Isis in relief in the delta marshes suckling Horus. The underside has four monkeys climbing a palm tree. 25th Dynasty. b) Steatite scarab with tiny body amid normal-sized legs. The underside has Bes and other magical figures, and the cartouche of Menkheperre. Ramesside. c) Steatite human-headed scaraboid. The underside shows a seated king and Maat. SIP to NK. d) Blue-green glazed steatite cowroid, with three *Tilapia* on the underside. NK. e) Blue-green glazed steatite cowroid, decorated with a lotus head and a *nefer*-sign. The underside shows Hathor as a cow in a boat in the marshes. NK. f) Steatite plaque with eight tiny scarabs. The underside shows *Tilapia*. NK. g) Steatite plaque with relief ram-sphinx. Amen-Re is named on the underside. NK to TIP. h) Steatite double rams' heads in disc and uraeus, separated by double *wedjat*-eyes. The underside has a sphinx and the name of Shabaka. 25th Dynasty, *c.* 710 BC. i) Turquoise-blue glazed-composition bundle-backed seal. The underside shows Seth and a falcon-headed god wearing a disc. L. 5.3 cm, NK.

human heads with carefully detailed hair and finely modelled features are also found. Of course, all the designs which appear on the underside of scarabs and scaraboids, and the shapes of the scaraboid backs themselves, can occur on rectangular **plaque** amulets, which could also serve as ring bezels. A popular form of scaraboid with a circular or elongated oval base and markings on its back which show that it is based on the cowrie shell is termed a **cowroid**.

55c

55d, e

Throughout the Middle Kingdom and Second Intermediate Period the range of designs on the underside of scarab amulets widened as more symbols were added to the repertoire and the possible combinations were thus increased. Elaborate floral designs of lotus, papyrus and *sma*-signs now often incorporated symbols of good luck or power such as the *ankh*, *nefer*, *ka*, the Red Crown and the bee. Indeed a large group of designs comprised nothing but hieroglyphic symbols such as the *wadj*-sceptre, *nub* (gold)-sign, *wedjat*-eye, scarab, *djed*-pillar, *kha*-sign and *was*-sceptre, frequently arranged in split mirror image and so combined as to appear almost capable of being read rather than just a decorative feature. In the same vein another group of contemporary scarabs bears 'fake' cartouches containing hieroglyphic signs in nonsensical arrangements. An important innovation is the large-scale figured scene, for in some at least deities are depicted; the Hathor head motif also becomes common. Also characteristic of the period are ever more complicated designs of scrolls and spirals, cross-patterns and rosettes, coiled and 'woven' patterns and concentric circles, often contained within a border of braided rope or spirals. Even the backs of some contemporary scarabs are decorative, with arrangements of scrolls and curls, spray-like branches and criss-cross patterns or heraldically opposed animals or birds on the prothorax and wing-cases.

During the earlier New Kingdom there were still some scarabs inscribed with the titles and names of their owners; these probably functioned as seals. The vast majority of scarabs, however, had the purely amuletic purpose of providing protection, attracting good luck or associating their wearers with desired powers or conditions. All these aims, of course, would be of as much use to the owner in the Afterlife as in the world of the living. Scenes with deities, like amulets in their shape, offered protection and demonstrated divine patronage or the wearer's special devotion. Not only are all the chief gods, goddesses and household deities represented (Bes is particularly popular), but those who are otherwise rarely, if at all, found as amuletic figures occur on scarabs. Hapy, the Nile god, with pendulous breasts and aquatic plants on his head, Astarte, the naked foreign goddess of love and war and Reshep, the Canaanite warrior god, fall within this category. Sometimes it is sufficient for just the name of a deity to be incorporated into a message: 'With Amen-Re behind (you) there can be no fear', 'May Mut grant a long lifetime' and 'Ptah rewards richly every good deed' are characteristic. Sometimes the god is not specified: 'May the god be content with all I have done'; 'Magnanimity is in god's hand (to give)'; 'May you have the favour of your god'. Occasionally the motto dispenses with the divine entirely: 'Happy New Year'; 'May your name endure, may your children reproduce'; 'Good luck'; 'I am true of heart'.

In the same way scarabs inscribed with just the names of kings have an obviously protective power, especially when accompanied by potent epithets such as 'smiter of the Nine Bows' (Egypt's traditional enemies), 'trampler of all foreign lands', 'maker of monuments' or 'establisher of laws'. Even the less aggressive epithets of a ruling queen such as Hatshepsut – 'sweet scent to perfume the gods of Thebes' and 'rich in offerings' – would still associate the scarab's owner with the world of the divine. Apart from the name of the reigning ruler those of long dead but especially powerful kings continued to be inscribed on scarabs, which has helped to confuse their dating yet further. The Old Kingdom pharaohs Khufu and Wenis were first inscribed on examples of New Kingdom date, not on contemporary ones. Apparently, as late as the Twenty-sixth Dynasty scarabs bear the throne name (Menkheperre) of Tuthmosis III of the Eighteenth Dynasty (*c.* 1479–1425 BC), who established the Egyptian Empire from the headwaters of the Euphrates to the fourth cataract in Nubia. Unfortunately this same royal name was borne by rulers of the Twenty-first and Twenty-fifth Dynasties, so the reference may be to them. In similar vein, no fewer than nineteen of Ramesses II's successors adopted his throne name Usermaatre. At least it is certain that when the Nineteenth Dynasty pharaohs Sety I and Ramesses II and Ramesses III of the Twentieth Dynasty chose to have the name Menkheperre inscribed on scarabs alongside their own, they were honouring their illustrious predecessor.

Probably even more efficacious, of course were figured scenes of kings, whether with their fellow deities, fighting from a chariot on the battlefield, executing Egypt's enemies, making offerings or just appearing in majesty. The last-named was a particularly favourite manifestation of Amenophis III on large-scale scarabs, often in the company of his wife Tiy. It was this king, of course, who issued a whole series of very large commemorative scarabs (between 5.2 and 11 cm long) recording in up to sixteen lines of text his marriage to Tiy, the arrival of a Mitannian princess with her retinue for the royal harem, the cutting of an artificial lake and the number of wild bulls and lions he personally hunted during the early part of his reign. Since examples have been found at sites outside Egypt their purpose has been likened to that of a commemorative medal, even a palace bulletin or newsletter to acquaint provincial administrators with the latest royal news. If this was their function, Amenophis was merely continuing on a grandiose scale a practice begun earlier in the dynasty and maintained during the early Ramesside Period. Tuthmosis III issued small scarabs recording the erection of his obelisks at Karnak;

Ramesses II recorded his eighth jubilee on scarabs. After the New Kingdom came to an end, scarabs with royal names become increasingly rare; the last known examples date to the final reigns of the Twenty-sixth Dynasty. Interestingly enough, the names of the kings of the last native Egyptian dynasties survive not on scarabs but on plaque or cartouche amulets.

Heart Scarabs

During the Old Kingdom it was considered enough to live according to a strict moral code to enjoy an Afterlife of bliss. During the troubled times of the First Intermediate Period, however, cemeteries were desecrated, bodies destroyed and the dead left unburied, so to prevent such terrible events ever happening again the belief was instilled that a man would be held responsible in the next world for his actions in this. To ascertain his worthiness to enter the Egyptian version of paradise he would be judged before Osiris, and part of the trial would entail the weighing of his heart which was considered to be the originator of all feelings and actions and the storehouse of their memory. As depicted in the vignette of Chapter 125 of the *Book of the Dead*, inside the great Hall of the Two Truths the heart was set in one pan of the balance and weighed against the figure of the goddess Maat, the embodiment of truth, justice, righteousness and cosmic order, or her emblem the ostrich feather. The accuracy of the balance was checked by jackal-headed Anubis in the presence of a panel of representative great gods and the weighing itself was watched nervously not just by the deceased but also by his *Ba*, his destiny and his birth goddesses. The result was recorded by Thoth and the deceased, now 'true of voice' (*mꜣʿ ḫrw*) – that is, 'not guilty' – was led before Osiris under whose rule he would spend eternity. Only this happy result is ever depicted, but always represented lurking alertly beside the scales was the hybrid monster Ammit with crocodile's forepart, lion's or panther's middle and hippopotamus's hindquarters. Her name means 'She who gobbles up' or, in one variant form, 'She who eats the dead', and clearly if the heart was proved to belong to a sinner she would eat it and the deceased would be denied an Afterlife.

However, at least as early as the Thirteenth Dynasty the Egyptians had invented the **heart scarab** as a magical means of preventing such a dire event; indeed it would allow anyone who possessed it to live a totally reprehensible life and still enter heaven. The heart scarab is so called because it was made solely to be placed within a mummy's wrappings, preferably bearing Chapter 30B of the *Book of the Dead*, the 'heart scarab formula', to bind the heart to silence during the weighing. 'Chapter to prevent the heart of the deceased creating opposition to him in the realm of the dead' is its full title, and the text at various points exhorts the heart 'not to stand up as witness', 'not to create opposition in the tribunal', 'not to be hostile in the presence of the Keeper of the Balance' and 'not to tell lies in the presence of the god'. It also specified that the heart scarab should be made from *nmḥf* (*nemehef*) a green stone which has not been identified with certainty; green jasper, serpentine and basalt have all been suggested. In fact heart scarabs are made from a wide range of green or dark-coloured materials, such as glazed steatite, schist, feldspar, haematite and obsidian; even blue-glazed composition, Egyptian blue, rock crystal, alabaster and red jasper occur. A suggested literal meaning of the name *nemehef* as 'it does not float' (that is, 'it sinks') raises the possibility that a heart full of virtue was expected not merely to balance against Maat but to pull the pan down. Although the scales are never depicted with the pans other than balanced, this could be due to the Egyptians' love of symmetry or a desire not to show the issue completely prejudged!

44

One of the earliest firmly dated heart scarabs belongs to a high official called Nebankh who is known to have lived during the reign of the Thirteenth Dynasty pharaoh Sobkhotep IV (*c.* 1710 BC). Made of dark green schist (siltstone), it has a human face where the scarab's head would be and a version of Chapter 30B incised on the underside with all the bird hieroglyphs rendered without legs, a characteristic of the period in funerary texts. Since hieroglyphs are pictorial, those in the shape of living creatures were believed to have the same capability as figured scenes of coming into three-dimensional being, so the relevant signs were rendered harmless for the tomb. For the same

44g

56 *Heart amulets.*
a) Green schist heart with characteristic markings. The underside has Chapter 30B of the *Book of the Dead* for the High Steward Kenna. NK. b) Green serpentine elongated heart and scarab combined. On top of the scarab is a prayer to sail across heaven and see the gods. On top of the heart are the emblems *tit*, *djed*, and *ankh*. The underside has Chapter 30B of the *Book of the Dead* for a man called Iwy. H. 9.8 cm, NK. c) Dolerite human-headed scarab on a heart-shaped base with traces of gold leaf on the legs. NK.

reason, some three hundred years earlier, two spectacular, large solid-silver scarab amulets from the burial of the Eleventh Dynasty Theban estate manager Wah were ritually 'killed' by having their eyes and mouths hammered and ripped before being set on the mummy. About 120 years after Nebankh, the Seventeenth Dynasty King Sobkemsaf II was also interred with a human-headed heart scarab, made from green jasper set in a gold funda inscribed with a version of Chapter 30B. This certainly suggests that there were earlier royal heart scarabs, now lost, for such an important amulet is unlikely to have been invented first for non-royal burials. The spell itself was reputed to be very old, having been found at Hermopolis beneath a statue of the local god Thoth by Prince Hordedef, son of the Fourth Dynasty pharaoh Menkaure who built the third pyramid at Giza, *c.* 2510 BC. But this looks suspiciously like a false pedigree, created for Chapter 30B to make it look older than it really was, a common practice to enhance spells and recipes. The text has no antecedent in the *Coffin Texts* and would actually be unnecessary before the First Intermediate Period. Other spells are also found on heart scarabs, especially 30A which differs from 30B in making no reference to the weighing, and also Chapter 26 of the *Book of the Dead* which is more often written on heart amulets (see Chapter 5). Conversely, of course, Chapter 30B frequently appears on heart amulets.

Not all heart scarabs bear a text, but they are usually recognisable from their material, the fact that they are unpierced and, most important, by their size: the largest are over 10cm long. On the other hand, one class of what can only be uninscribed schist heart scarabs are scarcely 3cm long. As has been seen, the earliest examples have human faces; other later fancy forms include a profile ram's head instead of the insect's and even a whole elaterid beetle's back instead of the scarab's. In some instances, the plinth on which the scarab crouches takes the shape of a heart, and a tiny human head in a tripartite wig is raised at a sharp angle to the insect's body. Indeed the scarab's back is sometimes decorated with the figure of one or more herons, just like some heart amulets (see Chapter 5). One class of very distinctive heart scarab, invariably of black steatite, is distinguishable by its uniform

front
ver c

56c

57 *Funerary scarabs with figured scenes.*
a) The underside of this steatite scarab shows Osiris standing between Isis and Nephthys. The decoration on the top surface is identical with that of b). Ramesside. b) The wing cases of this scarab are decorated with an incised seated falcon-headed sun god in disc and Osiris. Its prothorax has a full moon and cres- cent between *wedjat*-eyes. The underside shows Osiris between Isis and Nephthys. Steatite. L. 8.4 cm, Ramesside.

57 incised decoration. A falcon-headed sun god squats in one wing-case, Osiris in the other; in the prothorax and upside down to the figures is a celestial barque containing a full moon with crescent between *wedjat*-eyes. The only variant is that occasionally the sun god is replaced by a heron and the moon in the boat by a sun-disc. Although some of these examples have Chapter 30B on the underside, the majority have a large-scale figured scene of Osiris between Isis and Nephthys with a single row of text naming the deceased.

Occasionally heart scarabs were enclosed in 63 a gold funda or rim with a suspension loop for a gold torque or wire so that they could be hung around the mummy's neck. The wives of Tuthmosis III each owned a green schist heart scarab in a gold mount hung from a plain gold wire; at Tanis, Wendjebauendjed's green feldspar example was suspended by an articulated

58 *Funerary scarabs with holes for attachment to mummy bandages.*
a) Discoloured, turquoise-blue glazed-composition scarab, with moulded wings, and flat back. The scarab has been inlaid separately. W. 14.9 cm, Saite. b) Green-blue glazed-composition flat plaque with a moulded relief scarab on the top surface. L. 6.2 cm, LP. c) Bright turquoise-blue glazed-composition scarab on base with elaborately detailed free-standing legs and strongly convex underbody. Saite. d) Bright turquoise-blue scarab without legs, and with a flat underside. LP.

59 *Funerary scarabs with naturalistic undersides.* From LEFT to RIGHT
a) Haematite scarab with a ram's head. LP. b) Haematite scarab with a bull's head. LP. c) Lapis lazuli scarab with a falcon's head. L. 2.2 cm; LP. d) Diorite scarab; the underside has characteristic markings. G-R. e) In basalt, showing underside markings. L. 2.8 cm; G-R. f) In pale green glazed composition with a clearly visible loop for attachment to bandages. Saite. g) Pale turquoise-blue glazed-composition scarab with detailed back markings. The underside has a loop for attachment. Saite.

chain made from long gold tubes, one slightly curved for the back of the neck. Tutankhamun's heart scarab, however, was incorporated into a gold kiosk-shaped pectoral inlaid with cornelian and polychrome glass so that it lay between the figures of Isis and Nephthys. At Tanis, King Psusennes wore no less than four heart scarabs, but they were unframed: the setting for each was a large pair of vertical inlaid wings. That of Sheshonq II at the same site, however, was once again in an openwork inlaid gold pectoral, as was Wendjebauendjed's second example. This practice of inserting heart scarabs into a pectoral had devolved to non-royal burials by at least the reign of Ramesses II: two glass-inlaid gold examples naming his vizier Paser came from the burial of the Apis bulls at Saqqara. For most commoners, though, the heart scarab was usually inset into a solid but highly 47 coloured glazed composition (or less often, green-glazed steatite) pylon-shaped pectoral complete with cavetto cornice so that the insect's back was visible in one face and the inscribed underside in the other. The favoured setting for the scarab is in a boat between the figures of Isis and Nephthys or flanked by *djeds* and *tit*-amulets.

Funerary Scarabs

From the Twenty-fifth Dynasty onwards another variety of funerary scarab with wings is 58 very common. Usually quite large (5–6 cm is average for length), made almost exclusively from bright-blue-glazed composition and moulded with a flat underside, it was pierced by holes around the edge so that it could be front cover a stitched on to the mummy wrappings over the chest or incorporated into the bead net which enveloped contemporary mummies. The large horizontal wings, often with considerably detailed feathering, were made separately and attached at either side of the insect. A final category of small scarab with a funerary connotation is characteristic of the Twenty-sixth Dynasty and later and represents the insect naturalistically with its legs in high relief tucked underneath the highly convex belly. So 59d–g that it might be stitched to the mummy's wrappings, either a suspension loop lies at the centre of the underbelly or the underbelly itself is pierced from side to side. Examples of this type are made from finely modelled glazed composition, cornelian, lapis lazuli, haematite and diorite and are found in groups on the chests of Late Period mummies. A number of them have tiny rams', bulls' or falcons' heads instead of 59a–c the scarab's, but the symbolism is uncertain unless they were intended to link the deceased with the sun god in his ram and falcon forms and with the Apis bull as funerary deity.

5

Amulets of Assimilation

There can be little doubt that Egypt's earliest amuletic forms belong to what Petrie termed his homopoeic category. The belief in similars, whereby, for example, an eagle's feather was thought to confer on its wearer incredible fleetness or greatly enhanced vision, was prevalent in many ancient societies. In Egypt, too, only part of a creature was considered sufficient to represent the whole: amulets in the shape of antelopes' heads or birds' claws are among the earliest, found in burials of predynastic date before 3100 BC. However, just as early are amuletic images of complete animals whose qualities or characteristic behaviour the wearer may have wished to acquire by assimilation. Yet, particularly at this early time, there is always the possibility that when amulets take the form of a powerful or dangerous creature, they are intended to give protection by acting apotropaically – that is, to ward off the very creature which they represent pictorially (see Chapter 3).

Antelope/Oryx/Gazelle/Ibex

Although from a zoological point of view it ought to be possible to distinguish between these horned creatures, when they are in stylised amuletic form it is usually far from easy. The head of an antelope (or ibex, according to its excavator) is one of the earliest-known Egyptian amulets, shaped from bone and dating to the predynastic Badarian Period, *c.*4500 BC. Perhaps it was hoped that its wearer would be endowed with the animal's fleetness of foot or would by extension be rendered a great hunter of these desert creatures. Only later did the antelope become synonymous with evil, being one of the forms assumed by the god Seth and his henchmen. Were glazed-composition or steatite heads of Old Kingdom date, therefore, expected to act apotropaically, averting the very malevolence they embodied? Yet, well-modelled glazed-composition trussed antelopes, probably of New Kingdom date, might just as well represent a food offering. Moreover, during the New Kingdom, and particularly in the Ramesside Period, a three-dimensional crouched antelope or gazelle kneeling on an oval base, invariably of glazed steatite, occasionally served the same purpose as contemporary scarabs. The animal was also a popular subject for the plaque-shaped openwork bezels of polychrome glazed-composition finger-rings of the same period. It would appear that in this context the creature was believed to have regenerative powers: it lived successfully in the desert which was inimical to life and so had an ability to overcome the land of death and thus death itself. It is probably this symbolism which underlies the gold-foil ibexes and gazelles, their legs wide-flung in a flying gallop, in the openwork amuletic collar of Queen Aahhotep and the electrum gazelle heads attached to the diadem from the burial of the wives of Tuthmosis III. However, the unique repoussé sheet-gold walking oryx wearing a *tit*-amulet at its neck from a First Dynasty burial may represent the sacred animal of the sixteenth Upper Egyptian nome.

92a

54f

60 *Non-sacred animals.*
a) Cornelian kneeling calf, perhaps symbolic of regeneration. NK. b) Cornelian duck with turned-back head, representing a food offering or symbolising resurrection. L. 1.5 cm, NK. c) Red glazed-composition couchant calf, perhaps symbolic of rejuvenation. 18th Dynasty. d) Buff glazed-composition dog symbolising protection. Roman. e) Pale green glazed-composition hare, symbolic of fertility and regeneration. L. 4.4 cm, Saite. f) Grey-blue glazed-composition dog wearing a collar. NK.

Bull/Ox/Steer

Throughout Egyptian history the bull, revered for its savage strength, courage and virility, was the royal creature *par excellence*. Its tail, worn at the back of the belt, was an integral part of the king's regalia from at least the time of the unification, to judge from the scutiform schist commemorative slab known as the Narmer Palette. Narmer himself is even depicted there in one scene in the guise of a bull goring an enemy. Furthermore, from the Eighteenth Dynasty until the end of pharaonic history, the royal Horus name, the most ancient of the five forming the royal titulary, always began with the epithet *kꜣ nḫt*, (ka nakht), 'Mighty Bull'. Yet because of the curious dichotomy of viewpoint so well established in Egyptian thought, wild bulls could also be hunted and slain by the king. Amenophis III was proud to record in one series of his large commemorative scarabs how he hunted and slew no fewer than 96 wild bulls out of 170 during a two-day exercise. Most amulets of bulls, however, represent the sacred animal manifestation of a particular deity (see Chapter 2). Others are plainly connected with the funerary ritual and the provision of food offerings (see Chapter 7).

21a
19c

There still remain a few amulets in the form of a three-dimensional couchant calf lying either with head turned to face the viewer or gazing straight ahead. They are made of red-glazed composition or cornelian, probably dating from the New Kingdom, and the symbolism is possibly of rejuvenation.

60a, c

A crudely shaped frontal animal-head amulet found in predynastic burials and continuing into the early. Dynastic Period is characterised by two prominent round holes for eyes, sometimes inlaid, almost encircled by curved horns, with a downward-projecting muzzle or snout. Made from steatite, alabaster, amethyst, cornelian but in particular serpentine, it has been cautiously identified as a bull's head and was therefore presumably intended to confer the strength and virility of the animal on its wearer. Although it has been identified elsewhere as a ram's head, this would still have connotations of virility by assimilation.

70f

Cow

From earliest times the Egyptians considered the cow to embody all the most admired aspects of motherhood: she was fertile, protective and provided sustenance for her young. After slaughter, of course, she also provided food for humans. However, from an equally early period she was associated with the goddess Hathor and later with Isis and the sky goddess Mehweret (see Chapter 2). A thus far unique glazed steatite amulet of Old Kingdom date takes the shape of a cow with head turned back towards a milker. It might be assumed it was intended to encourage lactation in a woman who wore it in life, but as it came from a male burial perhaps it was hoped only to provide the deceased with a supply of milk to drink in the Other World. This piece provides a very good example of the extra difficulty attached to any attempt to interpret the function of an amulet which has not come from an excavated context.

21b 66c

Thin frontal bovine-head amulets with strongly curving lyre-shaped horns, known as *boukrania*, which are first found in predynastic graves, are usually identified as cows' heads and associated with Hathor or Bat, the goddess of the Seventh Upper Egyptian nome, who appears in this form at the top of the Narmer Palette. They are a particular feature of late Old Kingdom and early First Intermediate Period burials, made of glazed composition and so stylised as to be barely recognisable.

Dog

Amulets of reclining dogs with lop ears, or else with indeterminate ears but clearly wearing a collar, are a feature of burials of the late Old Kingdom and early First Intermediate Period, after which they virtually disappear. In such instances there can be no confusion with reclining lions, although in many cases both forms are so crudely made that distinction is almost impossible. They are most commonly made of ivory or bone, with some glazed composition and occasional cornelian and steatite. Dogs'-head amulets are almost exclusive to the late Old Kingdom and made of cornelian, pink limestone or glazed composition. Such canine amulets, especially those which may represent greyhounds, can only have been worn to endow their wearer with fleetness of foot, for although the Egyptians went so far as to give their dogs pet names, their essential function was to hunt, not to be household lap dogs.

4g 5e

In the Graeco-Roman Period, however, a new type of amulet appears, invariably of glazed composition, which shows the dog standing in profile but with head turned inquisitively toward the viewer. The animal resembles a chow, with a ruff and a tail curled on to its spine. Perhaps now the symbolism is protection, for it is obviously a guard dog.

60d

Fly

An amulet with a long history, already found in burials of the predynastic Naqada 2 Period before 3100 BC, is the stylised fly, *afef* (*‘ff*), always recognisable from its characteristic wing configuration even when the head is not clearly distinguished. The earliest examples are of stone, notably serpentine, and both glazed and unglazed steatite, but by the end of the Old Kingdom cornelian, lapis lazuli and glazed composition had been added to the repertoire. Amethyst flies date to the Middle Kingdom; examples of glass first make an appearance during the New Kingdom.

4b

However, the finest fly amulets are undoubtedly those of gold. Although a few flies of sheet gold have been found, rather surprisingly, in a First Intermediate Period context, they are most characteristic of the New Kingdom, for it was then that they formed part of an honorific award which originally rewarded military valour. Perhaps the underlying idea lay in the Egyptian fly's typical behaviour: the gold variety rewarded persistence in attacking the enemy. Queen Aahhotep's burial at Thebes contained three magnificent examples made from a sheet-gold plate cut into the outline of the wings with an additional moulded section bearing details representing the head and protuberent eyes. Other examples are of gold foil moulded over a core with the eyes, ridging around the neck, markings over the rump and striations on the wings carefully delineated. No fewer than thirty-three flies came from the burial of the wives of Tuthmosis III, each made in two parts, the top stamped into a mould with a base plate soldered on. Whole strings of smaller solid cast-gold flies with decorated upperside and flat underside are not uncommon. Aahhotep also owned two small flat sheet-electrum

48e 48c

examples; five others of gold came from the Gold Tomb in the Valley of the Kings.

It is difficult to know whether all gold flies of New Kingdom date, especially when they occur in numbers, should be viewed as representative of the military award, but those in other materials, particularly when they predate the New Kingdom, must be purely amuletic. The symbolism of the fly as amulet rather than award is even more obscure. Perhaps the wearer hoped to emulate its renowned fecundity; perhaps it was purely apotropaic, intended to keep at bay this most persistent and prevalent of Egyptian insects. However, what is to be made of those fly amulets where the head has been replaced by that of another crea- 41b ture such as a falcon, moreover one wearing a moon's crescent and disc with uraeus on its head and a *wedjat*-eye across its wings?

Frog/Toad

The Egyptians rarely made a clear enough distinction between their amulets of frogs and toads for it to be certain which was intended. Both were noted for their prolific breeding habits. During the first century AD the Roman writer Pliny the Elder transmitted the Egyptian belief that the frog was an example of spontaneous generation, self-created from the mud from which it emerged. This idea no doubt arose because of the numbers of baby frogs which must have appeared in the mud each year when the waters of the inundation receded. It is not surprising that the four male creator gods worshipped at Hermopolis had frogs' heads, just as their four female counterparts had snakes' heads – both were creatures symbolic of regeneration. During the New Kingdom the hieroglyph of a frog was used as a joke writing to be read as the signs *wḥm ʿnḫ* (wehem ankh), meaning 'living again', a well-wishing term written after the names of deceased persons. This connection with new life was even carried down to the Coptic Period when frogs appear on pottery lamps bearing the text 'I am the resurrection'.

Presumably, then, when placed on the mummy, a frog amulet was believed to have particular powers of regeneration. For the living, however, the frog offered fecundity by assimilation and was particularly worn by women not just as a pendant amulet but from the New Kingdom also as a swivelling ring bezel. In a particularly fine example the frog is of solid gold with wire legs and sits on a lozenge-shaped gold bezel whose edge is dec- 45h orated with a double row of gold granules. The underside is incised with a scorpion suggesting that the ring may have had a funerary purpose, as Serqet was the scorpion goddess who protected the dead. In another type of contemporary ring made of glazed composition the frog bezel is made all-in-one with the shank. 93b Sometimes, too, a group of three frogs or more might squat on a glazed composition spacer bar from a bracelet. Since it was in amphibian form that the goddess Heqat participated in the creation of the divine child, crouched beside the potter's wheel on which Khnum shaped the small naked immortal, all frog amulets might be intended to represent the goddess in her animal manifestation. Without an inscription naming her, however, it is impossible to be certain.

Although it is already found in burials of predynastic date, the frog amulet does not occur in numbers until the late Old Kingdom and First Intermediate Period and then it often takes a specialised form, crouching with head upraised and eyes popping on an oval base bearing a design, inscription or scene on 54b the underside, the whole serving as a seal. Although the frog-form seal was soon ousted by the scarab in popularity, it continued to be produced alongside the uninscribed frog amulet until the Late Dynastic Period; frog amulets in glass made in open-backed moulds are found as late as the Ptolemaic Period. When found in position on the mummy this amulet usually lies on the upper chest but has also been noted at the throat, groin and upper arm.

The materials used for frog amulets, usually naturalistically coloured, included green-glazed steatite, green- or yellow-glazed composition, frit and glass, feldspar and serpent- 28h ine, but lapis lazuli, amethyst, gold, black and white porphyry, cornelian, diorite and orange chalcedony also occur.

Hare

Amulets in the shape of a hare first occur in the late Old Kingdom to First Intermediate

Period, made of such materials as cornelian and ivory, and still appear (sporadically) in the New Kingdom. They were most popular, however, in the Late Period, when they were made exclusively (60e) of green-glazed composition with a suspension loop on the spine supporting the long erect ears. Very occasionally the base on which the animal crouches is decorated so the piece can function as a seal.

The hare was a desert dweller and thereby credited with powers of regeneration, but its swiftness of movement and the keenness of its senses were also well known; it was even believed to sleep with its eyes open. Its fecundity, of course, was proverbial. Thus a hare amulet could be worn in life to endow its wearer with fertility or rapidity of movement, or in death with the hope of rebirth. The latter symbolism probably underlies the alternating (69b) cast gold and silver hares which race at the flying gallop around an openwork amuletic bangle.

Hedgehog

A hedgehog amulet made from calcite and strung with beads to form an anklet was found in a Naqada 2 burial at Matmar dating to just before 3100 BC. From that date, throughout the pharaonic period, the hedgehog was an important motif: its head sometimes appeared at the prow of Old Kingdom funerary boats, and during the Late Period cosmetic containers were made in its rotund shape. Its chief period of popularity as an amulet, however, was the New (54a) Kingdom, when it is often portrayed standing characteristically squat, its bristles carefully delineated and its oval base inscribed so that it can serve as a seal. In a variant form the legs are (54g) long, the pointed head extended and the body raised away from the base so that a hoop beneath the neck and another under the tail provide both a support and a means of stringing.

The hedgehog seems to have had a connotation of rebirth, perhaps suggested by its reappearance after hibernation. It was also a desert creature, surviving outside the fertile valley in inhospitable conditions. As it had conquered the land of death, it was felt to have conquered death itself. Apart from the early stone examples, hedgehog amulets were made almost exclusively of green-glazed composition.

Hippopotamus

One of the earliest of all representational amulets, a shell hippopotamus with tethered (3b) legs from a Badarian burial, can only have been intended to act apotropaically, protecting its wearer by warding off the attentions of this dangerous and bad-tempered animal. It is particularly interesting that, because of its point of balance, when worn this amulet would represent the hippopotamus on its back and hence at its most vulnerable. Hippopotamus' (70d) heads may have had a similar function, or were perhaps intended to bestow on their wearer the river-horse's great strength. They were usually of glazed composition, less often ivory or lapis lazuli, and dated especially to the late Old Kingdom, though they occurred sporadically until the New Kingdom. The hippopotamus, too, is connected with regeneration. Not only (28c) did it live in the renewing waters of the Nile, it was also believed to make its noisy roaring at dawn and dusk, thus linking itself with the sun's passage and the symbolism of death and rebirth. This regenerative connection is presumably also to be seen in the semi-precious stone grazing examples of Middle Kingdom date and the seals of New Kingdom date in which the back is not in the shape of a scarab (54j) but of a reclining hippopotamus or even two, curled around to form a circle. For amulets of the female hippopotamus goddesses see Chapter 3.

Lion/Lioness

The difficulty in distinguishing between crudely shaped early recumbent lion and dog (4g) amulets has already been explained, but undoubted big cats are found at least as early as the late Old Kingdom, fashioned from glazed steatite and composition. They continued to be produced until the end of dynastic history, though just as often in semi-precious stones such as cornelian, feldspar, amethyst and lapis lazuli. Although all are depicted with a well-delineated mane and tail curled around the right haunch, there are two basically different types. One, always of glazed composition, has a

61 *Heart amulets.*
a) Serpentine convex-faced heart with Chapter 30B of the *Book of the Dead* on both sides for the royal scribe Nakhtamun. 18th Dynasty. b) Red glass flat-backed heart. NK. c) Obsidian heart with flattened faces, the upper side with a scarab originally inlaid. The underside has yellow-filled Chapter 30B of the *Book of the Dead* for the priest and scribe of the estate of Amun Shed-Khonsu. NK. d) Turquoise-blue, human-headed, in a black tripartite wig. Glazed composition. L. 6.1 cm; 19th Dynasty, from Abydos.
e) Basalt, convex faced, human-headed heart wearing an elaborate tripartite wig with a lotus over the top of the head. The *Ba* with outstretched wings was originally inlaid. The underside names Paser. Ramesside.
f) Polychrome, glazed-composition human-headed heart with convex upper surface attached to a turquoise-green flat plaque. The head is inlaid separately. There is a *Benu* bird on the chest and the underside bears Chapter 30B of the *Book of the Dead* in black glaze. 18th to 19th Dynasties.

62 *Early precious metal amulets.*
a) Sheet gold ibis on a standard. FIP, from Mostagedda. b) Hollow sheet gold sphinx. L. 1.3 cm, FIP, from Mostagedda. c) Gold foil vulture and cobra on baskets, and silver foil stylised Double Crown on a basket, strung with glazed-composition and steatite beads. FIP; from Abydos. d) Sheet gold Double Crown on a basket, strung with gold beads. FIP, from Qaw el-Kebir.

63 *Detail of a painting on a column in the tomb of Sennefer.* Sennefer, mayor of Thebes under king Amenophis II, is offered funerary jewellery by his wife Meryt: a gold and lapis lazuli heart scarab on a gold chain, a gold *tit* amulet, a gold *djed* and a red stone snake's head all strung together. Theban tomb 96, 18th Dynasty, *c.*1420 BC.

64 *Amulets of varied materials.*
FROM LEFT TO RIGHT a) Red glazed-composition, flat-backed, squatting Horus the Child with an Amarna-style side tress. H. 2.8 cm, 18th Dynasty. b) Sheet gold human-headed *ba* inlaid with glass and cornelian. W. 5 cm, Saite. c) Amethyst crouched female sphinx. MK. d) Bright blue glazed-composition plummet. LP. e) Haematite headrest. LP. f) Diorite seated cat of Bastet. H. 1.8 cm, TIP. g) Lapis lazuli harpoon. L. 3.4 cm, LP. h) Obsidian two fingers. L. 8.5 cm, LP. i) Dark Egyptian blue ram's head on a column. LD. j) Green feldspar crouched female sphinx. MK. k) Leaf green glazed-composition openwork cowrie. NK to TIP. l) Red jasper seated lion-headed goddess. LD. m) Egyptian blue standing monkey with baby. TIP. n) Cornelian and gold human-headed pesesh-kef. FIP, from Hu. o) Bright turquoise-blue glazed-composition combined *ankh* and *was*. H. 3.3 cm, NK. p) Electrum wire *sa*. MK. q) Turquoise-blue glazed-composition *tit*. Saite.

66 ABOVE *Glass amulets.*
a) Lavender blue flat-backed baboon in the attitude of adoration. Ptolemaic. b) Light turquoise-blue, flat-backed, convex-faced heart. NK. c) Red, flat-backed, kneeling cow wearing disc and feathers, possibly Hathor. Ptolemaic. d) Yellow plaque with a kneeling mourning Isis in relief. Ptolemaic. e) Turquoise-blue plaque with a relief broad collar with tie strings. Ptolemaic. f) Translucent emerald-green recumbent jackal of Anubis in relief. W. 5 cm, Ptolemaic, from Akhmim. g) Dark blue plaque with the fetish of Abydos in relief, a box believed to contain the head of Osiris, topped by feathers and disc on a pole. Ptolemaic. h) White and purple flat-backed walking ram. Ptolemaic. i) Modelled Thoeris in black with blobs of red and white. 18th to 19th Dynasties. j) White flat-backed very rare amulet of Seshat, goddess of writing, wearing characteristic 5-pointed emblem on the head and writing on a palm-rib. H. 5 cm, Ptolemaic. k) Polychrome black, yellow, green and white heart with slightly convex faces. H. 2.1 cm; 18th Dynasty. l) Green and blue flat-backed *serekh* name-bead surmounted by an archaic form falcon wearing plumes. Ptolemaic. m) Yellow and blue flat-backed upreared cobra. Ptolemaic.

65 LEFT *Glazed-composition flat-backed fruit and floral amuletic jewellery elements of the 18th to 19th Dynasties.*
a) Turquoise-blue date. b) Pale green lotus flower. c) Red and mauve poppy petal. d) Green date palm leaf. e) Yellow and purple mandrake fruit. f) White and yellow daisy. g) Yellow, white and purple lotus petal. h) Turquoise-blue daisy. i) Turquoise-blue dom palm leaf. L. 4.7 cm. j) Purple grape bunch. k) Red dom palm leaf. l) Turquoise-blue mandrake fruit. m) Turquoise-blue palmette. n) Turquoise-blue lotus seed-vessel or pomegranate. o) Green and purple thistle or corncockle. L. 2.9 cm. p) Blue-green triple blossomed flower.

67 *Amulets of Old Kingdom and First Intermediate Period date.*
a) Gold falcon with part of a necklace of gold and turquoise beads. L. 17.4 cm, 4th Dynasty, from Mostagedda. b) Amethyst falcon. c) Cornelian double lion's foreparts, joined. d) Pink limestone human face. e) Cornelian leg with foot. H. 1.9 cm. f) Cornelian hand. g) Olivine turtle. H. 1.3 cm.

68 Book of the Dead *prescribed amulets.* Vignettes of Chapters 155, 156, 29B and 166 of the *Book of the Dead* of the scribe Any illustrating a *djed* of gold, a *tit* of red jasper, a heart amulet of *sehert*-stone and a headrest. H. 5.5 cm, 19th Dynasty, *c.*1250 BC.

69 *Amuletic jewellery.*
a) The girdle elements comprise hollow cowrie shells, one with a tongue and groove closing device on the underside, beard or side-lock pendants, fish amulets (*nekhau*) and a *Heh* amulet, all of electrum. The lotus pendant is of silver inlaid with glass and cornelian. The beads are cornelian, amethyst, lapis lazuli, feldspar and electrum. L. 46.3 cm, 12th Dynasty and NK. b) The gold openwork bangle (centre) is inset with a frieze of amulets and amuletic animals alternatively of gold and silver. The procession comprises a snake, a turtle, *wedjats*, two fingers (?), *Bats*, *ankhs*, hares, baboons, falcons and two ancestor busts (?). D. (external) 8.3 cm, early 18th Dynasty.

suspension loop on the spine and never has a decorated base. It may be of significance that most are late in date, for in a Late Period papyrus a spell against snakes requires the words to be said 'over a lion of glazed composition threaded to red linen'. The other rests on a base rounded at the back and square cut at the front, which is nearly always inscribed to serve as a seal; suspension is by a longitudinal boring. 54k As with frogs and cats, lions sometimes form the bezel of finger rings made all-in-one with the shank. A feature of flat-backed glass lion amulets of the Ptolemaic Period is their relaxed posture: often the head turns towards the viewer, the body curves around and the front paws are nonchalantly crossed.

From as early as the Sixth Dynasty, however, until the Graeco-Roman Period, some of the finest lion amulets were made of gold. The treasures of the Twelfth Dynasty princesses contained superb hollow examples which served as bracelet elements: Sithathor and Sithathoriunet each owned four pairs; Mereret had two. But gold and even silver recumbent lions also occur in contemporary non-royal burials and continue to be found in non-royal contexts until the Late Dynastic Period: the burial of the Meroitic queen Amanishakheto also contained solid gold examples.

In the New Kingdom military valour could be rewarded with a lion of gold which undoubtedly symbolized fierceness and bravery. Early amulets in this form were presumably expected to endow their wearer with the same qualities, but later ones may have had a protective function like that of lion-form waterspouts in Late Period temples. In addition lions, like all desert dwellers, were believed to have regenerative capabilities. It is no accident that one of Tutankhamun's funerary beds and all embalming tables were in the shape of a lion; and it is probably this symbolism which underlies the gold-foil lions in the flying gallop which form part of Queen Aahhotep's open work amuletic collar. Some lion forms are connected with particular deities (see Chapter 2).

What have been termed leopard-head amulets but might just as well be lioness heads first occur in the late Old Kingdom and continue into the First Intermediate Period. They are three-dimensional and made almost exclu-

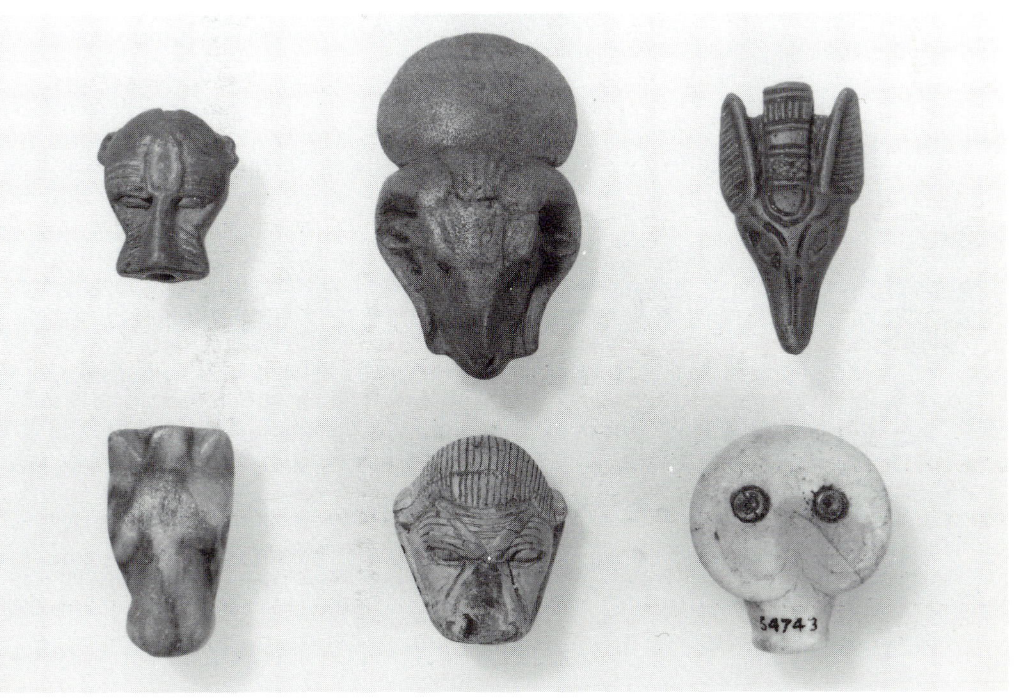

70 *Animal heads.* From LEFT to RIGHT
a) Dark green glazed-composition double-sided lioness head, pierced vertically. H. 2 cm, NK. b) Dark green glazed-composition flat-backed ram's head wearing a sun disc. H. 4.3 cm, TIP. c) Purple-blue glazed-composition jackal head. NK. d) Flat-backed hippopotamus head in mottled grey and white stone, possibly marble. MK. e) Colourless steatite scaraboid in the shape of a lioness's head whose underside names king Tuthmosis III. 18th Dynasty, *c.* 1450 BC. f) Alabaster bull's head with inlaid eyes of green glazed-steatite beads. Naqada 2.

5d sively from cornelian, although feldspar and limestone were also used. In the Twelfth Dynasty the treasures of the royal ladies Sithathoriunet and Mereret both contained girdle elements in the form of superbly modelled large hollow gold feline heads; Sithathoriunet also owned smaller quadruple examples. Again the big cat's regenerative capabilities must be the underlying symbolism. Although feline-head amulets continued to be produced until 70a, e the Late Period, the form changed into flat-backed examples of a high raised relief frontal head, made exclusively of glazed composition.

Claw-shaped amulets made of hard stone such as serpentine, not to mention real claws used amuletically, occur as early as the Predynastic Period and were still produced, though in different materials, in the Roman Period. They are a particular feature, however, of the Middle Kingdom: hollow or solid-gold examples came from the Twelfth Dynasty treasures of Sithathoriunet, Sithathor, Mereret and Khnumet, while electrum, silver and cornelian ones were excavated in contemporary non-royal burials. They are generally assumed to be leopard's claws, but those owned by Khnumet had the upper surface inlaid with turquoise, cornelian and lapis lazuli in cloisons to look like feathering, which surely suggests that a bird's claw was intended. Matched claw amulets, one on each leg, seem to have been a feature of women's anklets in this period: a dancing girl is depicted wearing them in a contemporary tomb at Qaw el-Kebir. Perhaps the speed or swooping actions of the bird were to be assimilated by the wearer; otherwise the symbolism is obscure.

Lizard

The lizard was symbolic of regeneration because of its ability to regrow limbs and tail if they were injured or lost. In this context it was placed on a par with the snake and that is why both are grasped by Underworld deities in scenes on coffins and funerary papyri of later New Kingdom date. Nevertheless, amulets shaped like a lizard are relatively rare. A collec- 48d tion of nineteen superbly modelled sheet-gold examples, each with suspension ring in the mouth and legs and tail spread as though sunbathing, are of New Kingdom date. A Twenty-sixth Dynasty green-glazed composition example shows two lizards modelled in the round stretched out side by side on top of a rectangular plaque. Small bronze reliquaries with suspension loops, surmounted by the figure of a lizard and intended to hold mummies of the reptile, were worn as a sign of devotion to the sun god Atum whose sacred creature they were.

Locust/Grasshopper

Amulets in the form of a locust or grasshopper, made from glazed steatite and glazed composition occur in both the late Old Kingdom and Eighteenth Dynasty and are carefully and naturalistically shaped. Yet a series of cornelian examples, probably contemporary with the former, are so stylised that they re- 5g semble a pair of aeroplane wings with only an inverted 'v' at the central point representing the legs and a few striations at the front for the head. Because of the reproductive qualities of this insect, the amulet probably bestowed fertility, although its swarming behaviour may also have led to connotations of plenty or riches. However, Utterances 467 and 627 of the *Pyramid Texts* both speak of ascent to heaven in the locust's or grasshopper's form, suggesting that the amulet had a purely funerary function.

Monkey (Vervet)/Maneless Baboon

Already in the late Old Kingdom rather crude amulets in steatite and glazed composition occur (in the Middle Kingdom they are characteristically of amethyst and cornelian) which 71a represent one of these simian forms; it is rarely possible to be sure which one is intended. Often it squats with head resting on paws, a posture which was revived in finely modelled glazed composition in the round during the New Kingdom. In other later examples of the same materials and occasionally also of cast bronze, it often stands upright, paws by its sides, supported by its long tail. It is this crea- 71c ture which is depicted in private tombs (particularly of New Kingdom date) under its owner's chair, where it is meant to serve not only as a pictorial record of a family pet but also as a symbol of love and sexual fulfilment to be enjoyed in the Other Life. Presumably this is

71 *Vervet monkeys.*
a) Amethyst figure squatting with paws on knees. MK. b) Deep Egyptian blue standing monkey holding its paws to its head with a baby at its feet. TIP. c) Pale turquoise-blue glazed-composition standing monkey, supported by its tail. H. 4.7 cm; TIP. d) Pale turquoise-blue glazed-composition figure, squatting, with a baby on its knees, wearing a *wedjat*-eye around its neck. TIP.

also its symbolism when it appears on the undersides of contemporary scarabs and forms 54c the sculpted backs of scaraboids. Perhaps this amulet, based on the creature's known sexual habits, was worn as a magical sexual aid in this world and the next. The examples which occur, always in glazed composition, of a squatting monkey holding a baby on its knees 71b, d or standing with a baby at its feet were pre- 64m sumably aimed at female wearers, as must have been amulets of heavily-maned dog-faced baboons squatting with their young. Although the latter were usually animal manifestations of the god Thoth, amulets of the creature walking on all fours, found as early as the First Intermediate Period, were presumably worn for their sexual connotations. Later examples, always of glazed composition or glass, in the 66a posture of adoration, would have been linked with rebirth.

Tilapia or *Bolti*

This fish shelters its eggs and even its hatched babies in its mouth and so for the Egyptians it was particularly symbolic of new life which appeared to originate from so unlikely an orifice. So potent was its symbolism that in one Ramesside workman's tomb at Deir el-Medina the deceased is represented as a gigantic *bolti* lying on a lion-form bier attended by Anubis. Generally tiny amuletic beads in its shape, made from green-glazed steatite and composi- 4j tion, cornelian, red jasper, feldspar and, later, 93c multicoloured glass and glazed composition, occur as early as the late Old Kingdom, but Middle Kingdom examples functioning as fish-shaped *nekhau* are of precious-metal 43a, c cloisonné work and the Eighteenth Dynasty burial of the wives of Tuthmosis III contained enough gold ones to form a triple stringed girdle. During the New Kingdom the backs of scaraboids were often carved into the shape of a 54h *bolti*; the fish was also a popular motif for the undersides of contemporary scarabs, usually in the company of other symbols of regeneration.

Ba

Ba is the name given to that uniquely Egyptian combination of human head on falcon's body which represents pictorially one of the three principal spirit forms which survived death. The word has been translated as 'soul', but it did not seem to convey that meaning to the Christian Egyptians (Copts) who preferred to use instead the Greek word 'psyche'. The *Ba* perhaps embodied the characteristics or personality of a man (or woman), the individual traits which distinguished him from all other human beings. It was the *Ba* which revisited the world of the living, travelled across the sky in the sun god's boat and anxiously witnessed the weighing of the heart in the Underworld lest, in spite of the heart scarab, the result prevented entry into the Egyptian paradise (see p. 56). Nevertheless the *Ba* always returned to the body in the tomb; indeed, Chapter 89 of the *Book of the Dead* is entitled 'Spell to cause the *Ba* to be reunited with its corpse in the necropolis', suggesting that if the *Ba* did not return willingly it would be coerced.

Amuletic jewellery in the shape of a *Ba* with outstretched wings does not occur before the burial of Tutankhamun. Found lying on the royal mummy's outermost shroud just below the hands, the earliest example is of gold with a flat back and depicts the head turned to the left; each claw holds a *shen*-sign of eternity. The bird's body and wings are a mass of cloisons inlaid with coloured glass representing feathering and, as befits a royal *Ba*, the human head wears a cobra on its brow. At Tanis, Prince Hornakht also owned a gold *Ba* amulet with outstretched wings, though only its head was inlaid. General Wendjebauendjed was interred with no fewer than four such amulets, but of sheet gold alone. As a variation, the wings of the miniature sheet-gold *Ba* amulet of King Psusennes I are curved above its head to form a tiny collar with all-in-one counterpoise. A few superb examples of gold *Bas* with outstretched wings and upper surface encrusted 72b, 6 with semi-precious stone inlays have survived from non-royal burials of Saite and Late Dynastic date, although sheet-gold or solid cast-gold ones with incised details are commoner. Another type of the same period made from sheet gold, glazed composition, lapis lazuli or flat-backed moulded glass represents the *Ba* 72a, 2 standing with closed wings. Both forms of this amulet, with wings extended and closed, are listed in the MacGregor Papyrus where they appear to be termed 'vultures with human 41a faces'. They were usually placed on the mummy in the general region of the chest and could presumably act as a substitute should the *Ba* refuse to return!

Apparently unique to Third Intermediate Period burials are amulets of twin *Ba*-birds standing side by side, often wearing sun discs, and modelled in the round from glazed composition. Perhaps they are an embodiment of the twin souls of Re and Osiris referred to in Chapter 17 of the *Book of the Dead* with whom the deceased wished to be associated.

Ka

Depicted pictorially as two upraised arms, this spirit form embodied the vital life-force or genius created at the birth of its owner as his

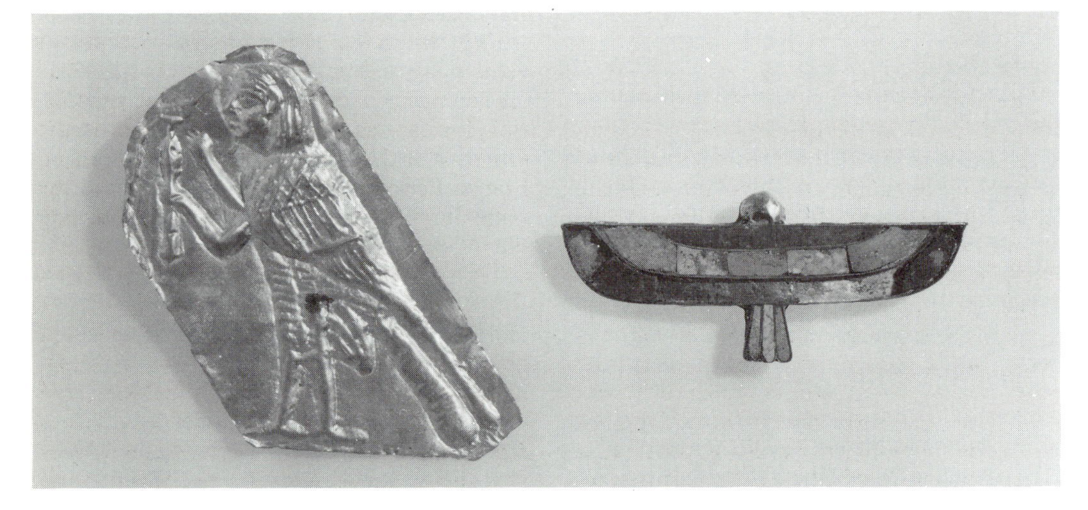

72 Ba-*birds*.
a) Sheet gold repoussé *Ba*-bird with a human head representing the characteristics and personality of the deceased, the figure pours a libation from a *hes* vase. H. 5.9 cm, LP. b) Sheet gold human-headed *Ba*-bird with a hollow modelled body on the underside. The back of the wings and tail are inlaid with lapis lazuli and turquoise. W. 5 cm, Saite.

double or twin, but with no separate existence of its own until after death. The *ka* was the recipient of food and drink offerings in the tomb which was sometimes called the house of the *ka*. Amulets in this form, known only from the Eighteenth Dynasty, may have acted as a substitute in case of destruction.

If an amulet shaped like an animal or part of an animal could bestow by assimilation its particular capabilities, so might those shaped like human parts, or less often whole human forms.

Mummy

Mummy is the term applied to the embalmed corpse which the Egyptians preserved by artificial means, first removing the brain and internal organs (except for the heart), drying out the empty shell, restuffing and anointing it, then wrapping it in hundreds of yards of linen bandages. It was hoped that by this process the dead would survive in recognisable form, for the Egyptians believed that, should the corpse perish, there could be no Afterlife. A number of chapters in the *Book of the Dead* are specifically concerned with preventing the corpse from putrefying in the realm of the dead. Thus an amulet depicting the mummy lying on its lion-form bier, sometimes attended by Anubis, the jackal-headed embalming god, represents a condition every Egyptian hoped to assimilate. All known examples date to the Ptolemaic Period and are made of glass or glazed composition in an open-backed mould. When found in position on the mummy, this amulet has been noted on the chest, lower torso and legs.

Parts of the Human Body

Amulets in the shape of parts of the human body or organs are characteristic of burials of the late Old Kingdom and First Intermediate Period, although a few had greater importance than others and continued to be made until the end of dynastic history. It should be remembered that although all these forms were intended to endow their wearer by assimilation with their particular bodily functions, they could also act as substitutes in the Other World should those bodily parts or organs be damaged or even destroyed. It has been suggested that the reason why most of them came to be no longer considered necessary was that improvements in the mummification process made limbs, in particular, less likely to become detached or injured.

For the sake of convenience these amulets will be dealt with from head to foot.

Face

Flat-backed front-facing heads are exclusive to the late Old Kingdom and First Intermediate Period. They vary considerably in quality of carving but almost all have a short beard, prominent ears and a projection on top of the head which is pierced from side to side for suspension. Although glazed composition, bone, limestone, steatite, ivory and even feldspar heads all occur, the predominant material is cornelian. Such an amulet was intended to give its wearer the use of the senses in general.

74c, 67d

74h

Eye

The unadorned human eye, as opposed to the *wedjat*-eye (see Chapter 3), occurs as early as the Fifth Dynasty in a burial at Mostagedda; it is made from openwork electrum. Thereafter, however, this form of amulet virtually disappears until the Late Period, when multiple examples are the norm. The earliest, probably predating the Twenty-fifth Dynasty, takes the form of a large convex disc, its top surface covered with relief eyes arranged in packed columns. Later in date are double and triple eyes standing one on top of the other. All are of glazed composition, in raised relief with details picked out in black. Mosaic glass examples, in triple units, are stylised into a lozenge shape with dark pupil on white ground, outlined in yellow and fringed by long dark lashes. The function of an eye amulet, reinforced by multiple forms, was the provisions of sight in the Other World. Gold-foil examples found on Roman Period mummies presumably had the same purpose in addition to that of protecting the organ on which they lay.

73a

73c

73b

Ear

Objects in the shape of a human ear, almost invariably of moulded glazed composition, pierced for suspension and of New Kingdom date, are usually identified as votive offerings rather than amulets. If indeed amuletic, their function would be to provide hearing.

73 *Human parts as amulets.* From LEFT to RIGHT
a) Turquoise-blue glazed-composition oval plaque with flat back and convex top showing columns of black-detailed multiple eyes in relief. The underside has a black-detailed *wedjat*. H. 6.5 cm, 25th Dynasty. b) Gold foil eye to guarantee and protect sight. Roman. c) Two-sided double eye with black details. Turquoise-blue glazed composition. LP. d) Gold foil tongue to guarantee speech and protect the mouth. Roman. e) Obsidian two fingers (perhaps the embalmer's) to reconfirm the mummification process and protect the embalming incision. L. 8.5 cm; LP.

Tongue

Gold-foil examples of tongue amulets were placed on Roman Period mummies' mouths, presumably to guarantee the faculty of speech, but perhaps also to protect the orifice from harmful forces which might seek to enter by it. 73d

Hand/Fist

74a Amulets in the shape of a hand or fist, pierced for suspension at the wrist, undoubtedly conferred dexterity and the power of manual activity. Often right and left can be distinguished; occasionally the underside is worked as carefully as the upperside, and even bracelets are depicted. Sometimes two fists jointed at the wrist are represented. When found in place on the corpse, open hands are invariably at the wrists, often strung with beads; curiously, the fist amulet does not appear to be fixed in position on the body. Both occur first in the Fifth Dynasty although they are a particular feature of First Intermediate Period burials, becoming progressively debased in form. Hand amulets, including a matched sheet-gold pair, are still found in the Middle Kingdom; individual ones have been identified in Middle Kingdom, New Kingdom and Third Intermediate Period contexts. Some finely detailed matched pairs of fists are said to date to the Eighteenth Dynasty. The material used for open hands and fists was predominently cornelian and, to a lesser extent, glazed composition, but ivory, bone, copper, limestone and steatite were also employed for the former, alabaster and feldspar for the latter. 74d 67f

74 *Human parts as amulets.* From LEFT to right
a) Dark green schist fist. OK. b) Turquoise-blue glazed-composition upraised human arms in relief, symbolising the *ka*, one of the spirit forms which survived death. 18th Dynasty. c) Bone two-faced beardless human head. FIP.
d) Cornelian flat-backed right hand. FIP. e) Cornelian modelled leg with foot. H. 2.5 cm, FIP. f) Cornelian right arm with fist. FIP.
g) Cornelian flat-backed leg with foot and bone buckle-beads imitating cowries. FIP, from Mostagedda. h) Cornelian flat-backed bearded human heads with gold and cornelian beads. OK to FIP.

Arm with Fist

Amulets in the form of an arm with fist, 74f pierced through the upper arm for suspension, are unique to the late Old Kingdom and First Intermediate Period and made almost exclusively of glazed composition. Although the type becomes so debased that the fist eventually vanishes completely, it was undoubtedly intended to confer the capability for any forceful activity.

Phallus

The phallus amulet, one of the forms depicted in the MacGregor Papyrus, was intended for the protection and magical preservation of the organ in question. Actual examples can show either the left or right side of the erect member. It is unique to and characteristic of the Late Period, made of serpentine, other dark-coloured hard stones or sheet gold; glazed composition and glass examples probably date to the Ptolemaic Period.

Leg with Foot

Amulets representing the foot and unbent leg as far as the knee are unique to the late Old

Kingdom and First Intermediate Period and are often found in matched pairs of one right and one left, especially strung with other elements such as buckle beads to form anklets. [74g] It has been noted that there are two forms: one is pierced from side to side and is least detailed; those with front-to-back piercing, however, almost invariably show the individual toes and [74e] greater naturalism. [67e] Again, both exhibit progressive debasement. Cornelian is by far the commonest material, although there are some examples of glazed composition, and even copper and ivory occur. This amulet's function was to bestow the power of movement or replace a lost limb.

Heart

To the Egyptians the heart was the most essential of organs, not because it pumped blood around the body – it is unclear that they understood this function – but because they believed it was the seat of intelligence, the originator of all feelings and actions, and the storehouse of memory. This is why it was the heart which was weighed in the balance in the Underworld to ascertain whether its owner was worthy to enter the Egyptian paradise: only it retained the memory of its owner's deeds upon earth. It is also why some heart amulets are inscribed with the so-called heart scarab formula (see p. 56). [56a, b] Alone among the internal organs removed from the corpse during mummification the heart was left in place within the body cavity; should it be accidentally removed, it was returned and stitched into place. [68] No less than four chapters of the *Book of the Dead* (numbers 27 to 29A) were concerned with 'not permitting a man's heart to be taken away in the realm of the dead'. Another, Chapter 26, is entitled 'Chapter for giving the deceased's heart to him in the realm of the dead'. Chapter 29B is specifically for 'a heart amulet of *sehert*-stone' (that is, the prescribed funerary amulet in the shape of a heart made from cornelian). The word used in this text makes it clear that the amulet was called *ib* even though there are other words for 'heart', such as *ḥ3ty* (haty), which is also used in the heart scarab formula.

Only two heart amulets are known which might predate the New Kingdom but their dating is uncertain, otherwise they do not occur earlier than the very time they first appear as prescribed funerary amulets in the *Book of the Dead*. Once established, however, the heart became one of the most important of all amulets and was set on every mummy until the end of the pharaonic period, often in numbers and usually on the upper torso. The Egyptians tended to depict the heart in the [61a,] form of an egg-shaped vessel, its greater width [66b] near the top, with a flat-topped rim surmounted by a ribbed suspension tube and what look like long lug handles. Some heart amulets are more rounded in outline; others, rather than ovoid, are lentoid or even flat, or at least flat-backed. The more naturalistic versions have an inverted crescent-shaped marking near the top [56a] above a hoop-shaped marking which lies immediately above the base. It has been suggested that all such features indicate the remnants of blood vessels whose position would have been known to the Egyptians from their butchery of animals. Indeed, the heart depicted as amulet or hieroglyph is usually identified as the animal rather than the human type. Certainly the bull's heart, which was one of the most important items presented to the mummified corpse during the Opening of the Mouth ceremony, carried out on the day of burial to restore to the deceased all his earthly faculties, is marked in exactly the same way. Presumably, then, the one type of heart known to the Egyptians was used to represent the human one too.

Heart amulets of New Kingdom date are still relatively rare; it has even been suggested, improbably, that one type, characteristic of the Eighteenth Dynasty and made from polychrome glass, [66k] does not represent a heart at all but a miniature vessel (see page 101). Two of the earliest securely dated non-royal examples with an almost round outline, modelled in wax, come from the burial of Akhenaten's vizier, Aper-el at Saqqara. Both have a *benu*-bird (heron) on the top surface. Tutankhamun, of course, owned an identical example, but of gold with inlay. Others with the same decoration, particularly made of glass or glazed composition, sometimes with the bird in a different [61f] colour, must be of a similar date. [100c] Being closely connected not only with the sun god, hence rebirth, but with the very creation of the world, the *benu*, sometimes erroneously referred to as a phoenix, was eminently suited to be found on a funerary amulet. Indeed, in Chapter 29B of the *Book of the Dead*, one of the texts especially associated with the heart amulet, the deceased says, 'I am the *benu*-bird, the *Ba* of Re.' The 61c relief scarabs which appear on the top surface of other heart amulets have an equally obvious regenerative symbolism. Since the Egyptian concept of the heart was that it encompassed the very essence of the deceased, his intelligence, feelings and memory, it is not surprising that a few examples are personified by being 61d–f crowned with a human head; some of them 61e even depict a *Ba*-bird stretching its wings across the central area of the amulet as though the heart were symbolically representing the man himself.

Although cornelian was stipulated for heart amulets, just about every material known to the Egyptians actually occurs. That red jasper, granite and glass should be employed is unsurprising, but green stones such as feldspar, olivine, serpentine, jasper (and glazed composition imitating them) were also used, as were lapis lazuli, blue glass and frit and dark-coloured hard stones such as obsidian, basalt, porphyry and haematite. The former can be explained by the fact that green is the colour of new vegetation and blue of the Nile's reviving waters; any hard stone has connotations of lasting for eternity. But the underlying symbolism of amethyst, steatite, limestone and alabaster, all of which occur, is uncertain.

A particularly fine set of eleven lapis lazuli hearts, gradated in size, some bound with gold, was found on the mummy of King Psusennes I at Tanis. One is on a long loop-in-loop gold chain, another on a gold ribbon; all bear the royal name and most have minutely and exquisitely carved figures of the three forms of the sun god. At the same site Amenemope owned two heart amulets of lapis lazuli and a third of rock crystal, superbly carved with the head of a baboon wearing a pectoral minutely incised with the king's name. The symbolism is presumably that the god Thoth, as recorder of the weighing of the heart, often took baboon form. In Saite non-royal burials, hearts of sheet gold with incised details or even solid cast gold are often found alongside cornelian examples.

A few instances are known of New Kingdom officials depicted wearing a heart amulet; however, in his tomb at Thebes the mayor Sennefer 63 is hardly ever without two which he wears side by side. Occasionally they are undecorated, sometimes they have the characteristic markings, but most often they bear the name of Amenophis II of the Eighteenth Dynasty, the king whom Sennefer served. Since Sennefer would not be expected to wear any heart but his own, perhaps there is a visual pun: in Egyptian the word for 'favourite' is *imy-ib* (literally 'the one who is in the heart'): in this case the king's heart. Wearing a heart with his monarch's name shows that Sennefer is his favourite.

6

Amulets of Powers

Petrie termed his second category of amulets dynatic; these are in the shape of, for the most part, inanimate objects which were imbued with authority and power, or else were representative of a certain condition, state or quality which the deceased desired to enjoy in the Afterlife. Not surprisingly, a number of them take the form of royal regalia like crowns and sceptres, or royal creatures like the cobra and sphinx. Their appearance marks the democratisation of funerary religion in Egypt. What had once been the prerogative of royalty and a few highly favoured courtiers was now available to all. This process reaches the peak of incongruity when the friezes of personal possessions depicted inside the coffins of commoners during the Middle Kingdom contain royal regalia almost as a matter of course. Other amulets in this category have divine or cosmic associations which again would originally have been intended solely for the promotion of the royal Afterlife. Some of the remainder are concerned with the funerary ritual.

Royal and Divine Powers

The beginning of the Dynastic Period in about 3100 BC was marked by the unification of the two predynastic kingdoms of Upper and Lower Egypt. On his palette Narmer is the first king thus far known to be depicted wearing the distinctive crown of each realm. As ruler of Upper Egypt, the land south of the delta, he wore the headgear known from its colour as the **White Crown**. Called in Egyptian *ḥḏt* (hedjet), 'White One', but also *wrt* (weret), 'Great One', it takes the form of a tall conical shape with a bulbous top and was probably made from starched linen or white leather over a wicker frame. Its white colour is all-important and invariable, yet, curiously, all the amulets in its shape without exception are green, whether of glazed composition or glass. Although it is the earlier of the two crowns ever to be depicted, single amulets in its shape are not found with certainty before the Saite Period when they are generally well formed in the round (even the ear-flaps are carefully delineated) with a suspension loop at the back. The **Red Crown**, however, worn by Narmer as king of conquered Lower Egypt (the delta), first appears in amuletic form as early as the First Intermediate Period. Its characteristic shape is a low cylinder with a tall spike at the back and an uncurling spiral projecting at the front. Called in Egyptian *dšrt* (deshret) 'Red One' (but also 'Great One', like the White Crown), the Red Crown was probably made from red-dyed linen or leather over a frame. Its colouring was invariable yet, apart from a few of the earliest examples which were carved from cornelian, amulets in its shape, like those of the White Crown, are usually of green-glazed composition. What is also surprising is the number of Red Crown amulets in burials of the First Intermediate Period which are made of gold, for the period is usually regarded as one of impoverishment. Sheet-gold examples are also able technically to represent the crown's spiral attachment as an independent feature, whereas those made from composition can depict only the filled-in outline of the crown including the spiral; suspension is by a

75c
75c
75b, d

75 *Amulets of royal and divine power.*
a) Leaf-green glazed-composition *was*-sceptre in the round, a symbol of divine power. LP. b) Turquoise-blue glazed-composition Red Crown of Lower Egypt, in the round. H. 2.9 cm, Saite. c) Turquoise-blue glazed-composition White Crown of Upper Egypt, in the round. Saite. d) Cornelian Red Crown, in the round. LP. e) Cast bronze *was*-sceptre. H. 5 cm, LP.

hole from front to back surface. After the First Intermediate Period, Red Crown amulets disappear until the Saite Period.

Early Red Crown amulets often represent the crown standing on a basket, the hieroglyphic *neb*-sign, perhaps the whole a rebus for 'Mistress of the Red Crown', personifying the crown as a powerful goddess. This would appear to be supported by the name for the **Double Crown**, the combination of the Red and White Crowns symbolising the united kingdoms, which was called in Egyptian *Sḫmty* (Sekhemty), the 'Two Powerful Ones'. Early amulets in the shape of the Double Crown often depict it also standing on the *neb* basket, and in the crudely formed examples of First Intermediate Period date made of glazed composition, it is not always possible to distinguish between the Red and the Double Crown. However, detailed gold examples of the same period can be clearly identified as Double Crowns. Curiously this amulet disappears after the First Intermediate Period. Only the White Crown is depicted among the amulets listed in the Osiris complex at Dendera, but that is probably because of its special association with the god of the dead.

62c, d

All three forms of crown would have been worn only by the king and certain deities, so amulets in their shape, when placed on the mummy of a commoner, would imbue him with the same aura of power and authority as pharaoh or god in the Other World. The **crook and flail**, too, were an essential part of the royal regalia carried by the king, either together or individually, in his double role of good shepherd and chastiser. Called in Egyptian *ḥḳ3t* (heqat) and *nḫḫ* (nekhekh) respectively, both are represented in the MacGregor Papyrus but actual examples are rare, being generally only of sheet gold and found on mummies of Late Period date.

16b

Although the royal wig cover with lappets and pigtail (the *nemes*) and the rarer *afnet* without lappets and pulled in at the nape to leave a broad band of cloth hanging at the back are both represented in the MacGregor Papyrus list, only one example of each amulet has been noted. The undated *afnet* is of cornelian with a suspension loop at the back; the grey stone (?) *nemes* from the Late Ptolemaic burial of a Buchis bull, sacred to Monthu, at Armant might be an inlay rather than an amulet.

16b

From the earliest dynasties the upreared cobra, the **uraeus**, was the emblem of royalty, worn on pharaoh's forehead to signify his kingship and divinity. As a goddess she was the eye of the sun, spitting fire at the king's enemies. Called in Egyptian *iʿrt* (iaret) or *mḥn* (mehen), 'the Coiled One', the uraeus was among the amulets depicted in both the Mac-

76 *Forms of uraei.*
a) Pale green glazed-composition uraeus with a single coil behind the base of the hood. Saite. b) Pale turquoise-blue glazed-composition uraeus. Saite. c) Flat-backed uraeus made of grey-green glass. Ptolemaic. d) Double bronze uraei wearing sun discs, inlaid with cornelian and blue and red glass. NK. e) Gold and electrum flat openwork uraeus on a basket. H. 5.3 cm, MK.

Gregor Papyrus and the Osiris complex at 1 Dendera. Usually more than one was placed on the mummy, sometimes at the forehead or even over the feet, but most often on the torso. The uraeus, which as amulet was intended to provide the non-royal dead with the protection usually reserved for royalty, but which, because of the sloughing of its skin also symbolised resurrection, exists in two basic forms from the Twenty-sixth Dynasty 76 onwards. In both the fully puffed-up hood is carefully detailed; in the commoner type a great coil of the body arches up behind to the same height as the head and has a suspension loop on top of it. In the other form only the tip of the tail appears to one side of the base of the hood which lies against a back pillar pierced for suspension. In fact uraeus amulets occur as early as the First Intermediate Period, but each one is idiosyncratically different whether carved from an almost undetailed lump of green stone or made from sheet gold with struts between the hood and tail. In the Late Period the materials used are as varied as 66m glazed composition, glass, gold, silver, bronze (sometimes inlaid), gilded wood, lapis lazuli and cornelian. Up to four uraei in a row, often perched on a basket, can form one amulet. For the various named snake goddesses who appear in amuletic form see Chapter 2; for the winged uraeus collar amulet see Chapter 7.

As early as the Archaic Period the **vulture and cobra** represented Nekhbet and Wadjyt, the patron goddesses of Upper and Lower Egypt who together symbolised the unification of the two predynastic kingdoms. This was their function when attached to the front of the royal headgear. Even one of the names in the royal titulary, the *nebty* or 'Two Ladies' name, was borne specifically under the goddesses' protection. Hence an amulet in this form would afford the highest protection to its wearer. In line with the democratisation of funerary beliefs during the First Intermediate Period, the vulture-and-cobra amulet first 62c occurs then in non-royal burials, almost invariably made of sheet gold with each deity seated on an individual basket. Thereafter the type disappears until the Saite Period, when glazed-composition examples are also found. Tutankhamun owned a full-sized funerary collar in the form of the vulture and cobra side by side with outstretched wings; it was cut from thin sheet gold with a matching counterpoise which was imitated in miniature by a tiny sheet gold amulet – one of a series – found on the mummy of King Psusennes I at Tanis more than 300 years later (see Chapter 7).

The ***shen*****-sign**, in Egyptian actually *šnw* 77a (shenu), was formed from a length of papyrus rope looped around into a circle with additional binding along the lower edge. Symbolically it represented everything the sun encircled during the course of twenty-four hours – in other words, the universe – but the *shen* also had

77 *Protective amulets.*
a) Pale green glazed-composition two-faced *shen*-sign. H. 3.7 cm, Saite. b) Empty cartouche made of schist and surmounted by feathers. LP. c) Lapis lazuli empty cartouche. LP. d) Cornelian *sweret* bead inscribed for the Treasury Overseer Amenhotep. NK

connotations of protecting what was within it in its function of a magical knot. It is this protective element which underlies the carrying of the *shen* in the back claws of such creatures as the *Ba*, falcon and vulture. It is not surprising, therefore, that by the time of the Old Kingdom, pharaoh's throne name, that is, the one he adopted on becoming king (and later too his given name as Son of Re) were both written inside an elongated *shen* called in modern times a **cartouche**, from the French word for 'cartridge', describing a decorative architectural feature. Thus, pictorially, pharaoh set his name on the whole universe and symbolically extended his control over it. The protective element, of course, was no less important. Possession of either amulet, but preferably both, would grant the deceased similar universal power and protection.

Although the whole point of a cartouche is that it should contain a name, any small ornament in its shape bearing a royal name does not function as a funerary amulet unless it comes from the burial of the king in question. Normally such cartouche ornaments with royal names would have been worn in life by officials of that reign as a badge of favour or else, just like glazed-composition signet rings bearing royal names, they were dispensed by the handful at festivals. Blank cartouche ornaments, however, were worn by the mummies of commoners, their form alone being sufficient to bestow their powers. Both *shen*- and cartouche-amulets are a feature of non-royal burials of the Twenty-sixth Dynasty and later, although the Twelfth Dynasty burial of Senebtisy contained a superb gold *shen* inlaid with cornelian and glazed composition, and similar examples were owned by the contemporary princesses Khnumet, Sithathoriunet and Mereret. Sometimes the cartouche is double, reflecting the fact that two of the five names in the royal titulary were written in cartouches; sometimes too it is surmounted by two tall ostrich plumes, occasionally with a sun disc between them, affording even greater protection. *Shen*-amulets are almost invariably carved from dark stone such as basalt, diorite and steatite, although a few in feldspar, lapis lazuli and green-glazed composition (always the most detailed) are known. On the other hand, lapis lazuli (also imitated by blue glass) is the commonest material for the cartouche, with dark stone the next most popular. Of the two amulets only the cartouche is represented among those depicted in the Osiris complex at Dendera. When found in position on the mummy, it usually lies on the upper torso with the *shen* somewhere in the vicinity.

77b

77c

The earliest title of the king of Upper and Lower Egypt, *nsw bity* (nesu bity), which is usually translated as 'He of the reed and he of the bee', was written at all times with the hieroglyphic signs of the reed and bee. Thus symbolically the insect had a significance far beyond its entomological importance. Amulets

41 in the shape of the **bee** are unique to the late Old Kingdom and First Intermediate Period and would appear to provide further evidence of the democratisation of funerary beliefs which allowed commoners to be buried with royal insignia. A few openwork examples are of glazed composition or sheet gold, which allowed individual details to be added as separate pieces of metal, but most take the form of a solid mass of cornelian, serpentine, limestone or glazed composition with only rudimentary details. However, the characteristic outline of the bee's wings and abdomen make identification certain even in debased types.

Perhaps the most famous monument to have survived from ancient Egypt is the great sphinx which crouches beside the Valley Temple of the second pyramid at Giza. This particular recumbent lion with royal human head (in this instance having the features of King Khafre) became inextricably identified in ancient Egyptian eyes with the protective Horemakhet (Greek Harmachis), 'Horus in the Horizon', a manifestation of the sun god believed to guard the Giza necropolis. The sphinx form itself, however, was essentially symbolic of the majesty and power of the king.

The earliest firmly dated recumbent **sphinx** amulet comes from a First Intermediate Period 62b burial at Mostagedda. It is formed from a sheet-gold cylinder with a flattened extension at the front representing the forepaws. The solid-cast head with roughly incised features and wearing a short wig has been soldered on; the back legs are delineated and the tail arches up to join the back of the head. Sphinx amulets are a feature of the Middle and New Kingdoms, made without exception of gold or semi- 48a precious stones such as cornelian, red jasper and lapis lazuli. In the Late Period, glass examples formed in an open-backed mould make an appearance, sometimes depicting the animal with human arms holding an offering vessel. Amulets in sphinx form linked the wearer not only with the protective power and authority of pharaoh but also with the underlying savagery of the big cat.

An amulet which is characteristic of the Middle Kingdom, although it first appears in the late Old Kingdom, has been termed a (proto)-*Ba* or, with more accuracy, a **female sphinx**. It takes the form of a very hunched, apparently crouched figure with elongated upraised human head wearing a tripartite wig. Details of the body are always sketchy, but it appears to be that of a lion. In the Middle Kingdom the materials used are invariably amethyst, feldspar and cornelian with some 78b,c lapis lazuli and serpentine; the stringing hole runs through the body from front to back. The earliest Old Kingdom examples, however,

78 *Female sphinxes.*
a) Red glazed-composition seated sphinx, with 'Nubian' four stranded hair style. 18th Dynasty.
b) Green feldspar crouched sphinx. MK.
c) Amethyst crouched sphinx. MK. d) Turquoise-blue glazed-composition seated sphinx, again with 'Nubian' four-stranded hair style. H. 3 cm; TIP.

79 *Sphinx-form deities.*
a) Grass-green glazed-composition unique Bes-headed figure wearing characteristic plumes. LP. b) Green glazed-composition snake-headed figure, perhaps Nehebkau, with threading holes through the base. TIP. c) Wooden Seth animal. The inscription around the base has an offering formula naming the god with unusual epithets. H. 5.7 cm, Ramesside.

whether shaped from ivory, limestone or glazed composition, clearly show that originally the body was a lion's and it is seated with the front legs vertical; suspension is by a loop on the spine.

An identically postured, well-modelled green-glazed composition version reappears at least in the late Third Intermediate Period, but this sports a curious hair-style consisting of four tresses emerging from the shaven crown to lie at the front, back and down each side of the head. Termed the Nubian style, it is particularly worn by young women in connection with birth, nursing babies and the putting on of cosmetics. Now, however, the body is clearly that of a cat, occasionally a nursing cat; indeed, sometimes a kitten sits between her paws. Undoubtedly the association is with the goddess Bastet. The only firmly dated excavated example of this amulet comes from the burial of a Kushite queen at Kurru dated to the Twenty-fifth Dynasty, but a unique red-glazed composition one may be contemporary with the only known relief of such a sphinx at Armant, said to date to the Eighteenth Dynasty. (78d, 78a)

During the New Kingdom and Saite Period examples of sphinx amulets in both recumbent and seated forms sometimes have the human head replaced by that of a falcon; the technical term is **hieracosphinx**. This is a manifestation of the Theban war god Monthu and is dealt with in Chapter 2, as is the **criosphinx** in which the head has been replaced by that of a ram and represents Amen-Re. In one rare glazed-composition seated sphinx amulet the head is that of a leonine Bes wearing his characteristic tall plumed head-dress (see page 39). (41d, 55g, 79a)

An amulet in the shape of a **lion's forepart**, made of cornelian (except for one known example in feldspar) and unique to the late Old Kingdom and First Intermediate Period, is specifically required by *Coffin Text* number 83:

> Words to be spoken over the forepart of a lion made of cornelian (or vulture's bone) and set at the neck of a man when he descends into the world of the dead . . . Thus will he have power over the four winds of heaven and become an excellent spirit as king of all the winds of heaven. As for every man who knows this spell, he shall not die a second time; his enemies shall not prevail over him; magic will never restrain him on earth. It means coming forth at his desire from the realm of the dead; it means becoming an excellent spirit in the presence of Osiris. (5b)

The powers of this amulet surely need no further amplification!

A **harpoon** as amulet represents the weapon carried by Horus of Edfu and his namesake, son of Osiris, when they opposed an enemy in the form of a hippopotamus. Dating exclu- (80a, 64g)

80 *Harpooning amulets.*
a) Lapis lazuli harpoon with bifurcated shaft-end. The point has a falcon head wearing a disc and uraeus. H. 3.4 cm, LP. b) Bronze falcon-headed Horus in Double Crown harpooning a hippopotamus. LP. c) Bronze harpoon with bifurcated shaft-end. The point, shaped like a falcon with downward-pointing wings, surmounts a falcon's head wearing a uraeus. L. 5.4 cm, LP.

sively to the Late Period, the finest, most detailed examples are of cast bronze showing the large pointed head, long conical shaft surmounted by the falcon-head of Horus and bifurcated end. Possession of one would grant the deceased the victory of Horus the Harpooner over the archembodiment of evil. (80c)

The *w3s*-**sceptre** (*was*-**sceptre**) which was carried only by deities, is recognisable from the long-eared animal-head set aslant the top and the bifurcated end of its long shaft. It is represented among the MacGregor Papyrus amulets, and examples in green-glazed composition, bronze, gold and gilded wood date almost exclusively to the Saite Period and later, although one in gold came from the Twenty-second Dynasty burial of Hornakht at Tanis. As a hieroglyph *was* wrote the word 'dominion'; hence an amulet in its shape would grant the deceased identical control in the Other World. (16b) (75a, e)

A number of Egyptian gods, most notably Amen-Re, the king of the gods, wore on the head as part of a composite crown two tall feathers called in Egyptian *šwty* (*shuty*). There is every indication that these feathers were **falcon plumes**, a well-known graphic representation of the unrepresentable, namely the (81a, b)

81 *Feathered amulets.*
a) Steatite double plumes with the feathering shown. LP.
b) Steatite double plumes. LP. c) Lapis lazuli double ostrich plumes. H. 3 cm, LP. d) Dark brown glazed-composition uterus-shaped (?) amulet with flat back. This emblem, worn on the heads of certain deities, was often replaced by two feathers as early as the Old Kingdom. LP. e) Pale turquoise-blue glazed-composition double ostrich feathers with sun disc. LP.
f) Gilded wood ostrich feather. G-R.

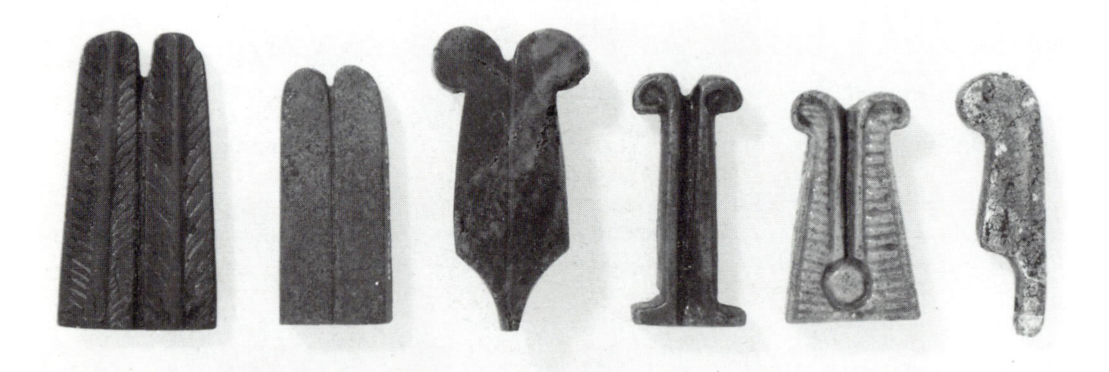

wind. Amun, of course, was originally a wind god at Hermopolis. So far as the amuletic form is concerned, there is evident confusion between the two plumes and the double **ostrich feathers** which are usually found flanking the White Crown, converting it into an *atef*-crown, but were sometimes worn on their own, especially in the Late Period, the time when both these amulets first occur. The visual difference is that in Egyptian iconography an ostrich feather is depicted with a characteristically curled-over top and a single stem running down one edge; a falcon's plume has a rounded tip and, when there is sufficient detail, the stem runs down its centre. In the best examples ostrich feathers also have an inverted pyramidal base, but often both types of amulet have a flat lower edge. A surprising range of mainly dark-coloured stones was used in these amulets' manufacture with serpentine, green porphyry and feldspar predominating for falcon plumes and obsidian and basalt for ostrich feathers, although both forms are also found in lapis lazuli and limestone. Suspension was through a loop at the back or at the base (so the piece would have hung upside down), or by a hole running from front to back. The wearer of a double-plumes amulet would have been imbued with divine dignity and majesty.

81f

81a

81c, e

One of the most ancient deities was the goddess Neith, whose main cult centre was at Sais in the delta. In the First Dynasty queens' names were already compounded with hers and a pendant jewellery element took the form of her sacred creature, the elaterid beetle. As befits so ancient a goddess, Neith herself and her name could be represented pictorially by her fetish, the earlier form a curious figure-of-eight object, perhaps a shield, with two arrows crossed behind it. The **fetish of Neith** as amulet, however, which does not occur before the Twenty-sixty Dynasty, represents two bows tied together, a version which had long since ousted the original fetish in most other sources. Often there is a total lack of internal detail, the outline reduced to two fish-tail ends and two long convex sides. The varied materials from which they were made include glazed composition, cornelian, agate, alabaster, limestone, onyx and quartz. Since Neith was one of the four goddesses who protected the dead, her amulet would provide the deceased with specialist protection but also link him with her warlike power and ancient majesty.

5c

82a, c

Amulets of the **sistrum** (rattle), generally of glazed composition, exclusive to the Twenty-sixth Dynasty and later, associated their wearer with the powerful goddess Hathor (see page 19) in her aspect of bringer of music and joy.

82d

To the Egyptians the green of fresh vegetation which symbolised new life and, by extension, resurrection, was exemplified by the

82 *Divine power and music.*
a) Solid-cast gold stirrup-shaped signet ring, the bezel in the shape of the fetish of Neith, incised with the figure of the goddess in the Red Crown. Saite. b) Solid-cast gold sistrum handle surmounted by a double faced Hathor head. MK. c) Agate fetish of Neith representing two bows tied together. LP. d) Grass green glazed-composition flat-backed openwork sistrum composed of a shrine containing a uraeus between the horns surmounting head of Hathor. H. 4 cm, TIP. e) Bright turquoise-blue glazed-composition lyre with gazelle head supports. TIP. f) Turquoise-blue glazed-composition cow's horns and disc. Saite.

83 *Papyrus sceptres.*
a) Green feldspar plaque with a naturalistic relief *wadj*. Saite. b) Pale turquoise-blue glazed-composition *wadj* in the round with basal leaves, head markings and shaft bindings delineated. Saite. c) Green feldspar *wadj* with unintelligible text. H. 7.4 cm; Saite. d) Grey-green glazed-composition plaque with a stylised *wadj* in relief. H. 3.5 cm, LP. e) Green feldspar plaque with a stylised double *wadj* in relief. LP.

papyrus plant which, as the ***wadj*** or **papyrus sceptre** in amuletic form, was first mentioned in *Coffin Text* no. 106. By the time the *Book of the Dead* was compiled it had become a prescribed amulet. Both Chapters 159 and 160 concern a papyrus column of feldspar to be placed at the throat of the deceased: 'If it is sound, I am healthy; if it is undamaged, I am uninjured; if it is not struck, I am unwounded ... my limbs shall not become dried out.' The accompanying vignettes represent the amulet either as an individual papyrus column, or – especially in Late Period papyri – as a plaque with a column (or two) incised on it or carved upon it in raised relief. Examples of both types exist and, although their colour is predominantly green, glazed composition occurs as often as feldspar with some glass and glazed steatite; gilded wood, haematite and even cornelian were also employed.

83d, e

Most individual columns are shaped in the round with characteristically sagging shaft, sometimes with basal leaves defined, and open spreading head with suspension loop on top of it or just behind it. Some of the most detailed indicate binding at the top of the shaft, which suggests that a papyrus-form architectural column rather than the plant is represented. One of the earliest firmly dated *wadj*-amulets was found in the tomb of Akhenaten's vizier, Aper-el, at Saqqara; Tutankhamun's were of feldspar mounted in gold. Thereafter the amulet occurs sporadically throughout the New Kingdom and Third Intermediate Period, but most date to the Twenty-sixth Dynasty and later; the plaque form, like its occurrence in contemporary funerary papyrus vignettes, is characteristic of the Late Period. A papyrus sceptre was often carried by goddesses and the plant was the emblem of Lower Egypt and its patroness Wadjyt; hence its amuletic form not only guaranteed the wearer rejuvenation, it also linked him with the divine and in particular one of the great protective goddesses. Papyrus column amulets surmounted by a cat or a falcon-head may symbolise respectively a syncretistic form of Bastet and Wadjyt and Horus in the Delta marshes where he was reared.

29b

A ***djed*-pillar** is an amulet in the form of the hieroglyphic sign which means 'enduring', 'stable' and similar concepts. In shape it consists of a tall broad shaft crossed near the top by four short horizontal bars. Originally, it may have represented a stylised tree trunk with the branches lopped off. Certainly, when it first appears in connection with the rites for Sokaris, the funerary god of Memphis, and later for Ptah, the more powerful god of the same area, it was the central feature of the ceremony known as 'the Raising of the *Djed*'. Since this entailed the setting upright of a huge *djed* by means of ropes rather in the manner of a maypole, the tree-trunk origin seems highly likely. Later, however, Osiris adopted the *djed* as one of his symbols and, from that time

84

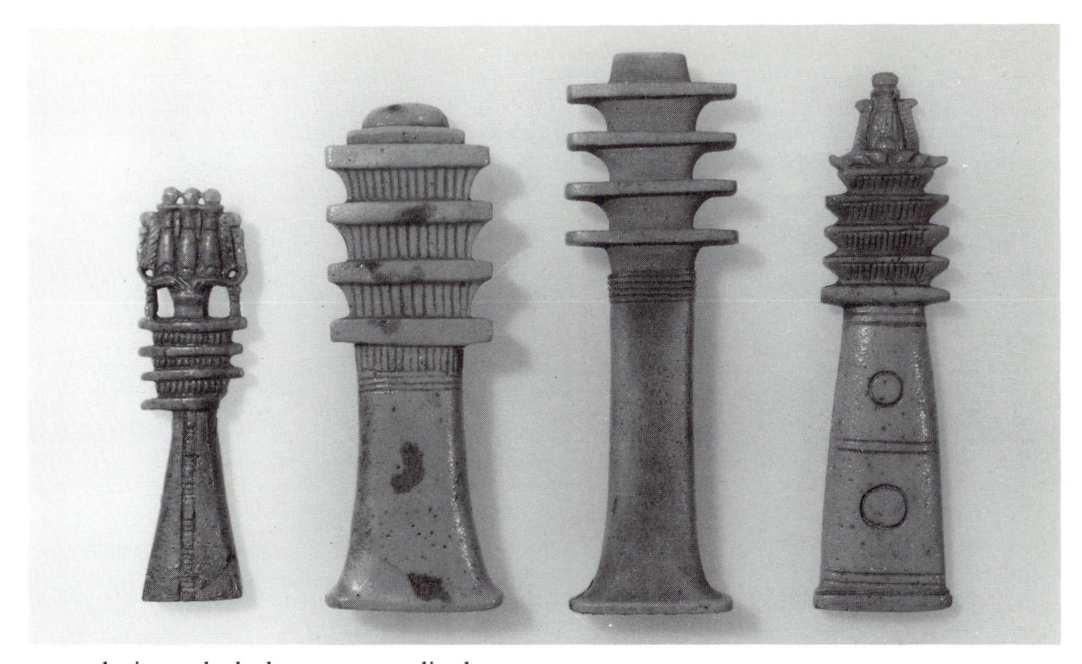

84 Djed-*pillars*.
a) Blue-green glazed-composition *djed*-pillar wearing triple *atef*. L.P. b) and c) *Djed*-pillars in turquoise-blue glazed composition, LP and Saite. d) Turquoise-blue glazed composition wearing *atef*. H. 11.1 cm, Ptolemaic.

onwards, it was looked upon as a stylised representation of the god's backbone. Indeed some Late Period *djeds* are further identified with the god by being surmounted with his *atef*-crown; extremely rare examples are actually animated by having human arms attached which hold *was*-sceptres. Moreover, Chapter 155 of the *Book of the Dead*, which concerns 'words to be spoken over a *djed*-pillar of gold strung upon a fibre of sycamore . . . and placed at the throat of the deceased on the day of burial', mentions only Osiris. 'Raise yourself up Osiris! You have your backbone once more, O Weary-hearted One; you have your vertebrae!'

68
63

The *djed*-pillar first appears in the Third Dynasty as an openwork decorative architectural feature at the top of a wall in the building west of the Hebsed Court of the Step Pyramid enclosure at Saqqara. Its first known occurrence as an amulet, however, is nearly five hundred years later in the late Old Kingdom, but thereafter it is one of the most common of all funerary amulets, usually found in numbers on a mummy and almost invariably strung out across the lower torso. In spite of gold being the prescribed material, many examples are of green-glazed composition or glass (and during the First Intermediate Period glazed steatite), with blue composition and glass and lapis lazuli not far behind. Both are the colours of regeneration. However, a significant number are also made of cornelian, another material with connotations of new life. Yellow-glazed composition was probably a cheap imitation of gold. One of Tutankhamun's *djed* amulets was of the prescribed material, another of gold inlaid with blue glass; all the royal burials at Tanis contained sheet gold *djeds*. The possessor of this amulet 'will be a worthy spirit who will be in the realm of the dead on New Year's Day like those who are in the train of Osiris'.

71
100b

Ritual Implements

The Opening of the Mouth ceremony carried out on the mummy on the day of burial to restore to the deceased all his earthly faculties and reincorporate the spirit within the body entailed the use of various prescribed ritual implements, among them the distinctly shaped ***pesesh-kef***. This object is characterised by a bifurcated shaft in which the two ends are upward-curving into points; perhaps the original was a fish-tailed flint of predynastic type, thus stressing the antiquity of the ritual. The earliest, most elaborate *pesesh-kef* amulets are unique to burials of the First Intermediate

85 Pesesh-kefs.
a) *Pesesh-kef* in steatite with a fish-tailed end and central groove. LD. b) Steatite *pesesh-kef* with stylised markings. L. 4.3 cm, LD. c) Dark blue glass *pesesh-kef* in relief on a plaque. Ptolemaic.
d) Cornelian fish-tailed blade surmounted by gold human-headed handle FIP, from Hu.

Period and early Middle Kingdom and have a 85d bewigged human head at one end of a flat blade 64n which ends in two upward-curving points. In particularly fine examples the head and blade are of different materials such as gold and cornelian or silver and copper. From the New Kingdom, however, the form no longer has the human head and is made from dark-coloured stones such as obsidian, basalt and serpentine. One of the earliest examples of this type, made from steatite, was found on the mummy of Tjuya, grandmother of Akhenaten, whose burial was in the Valley of the Kings. Most *pesesh-kef* amulets come from non-royal burials of the Twenty-sixth Dynasty and later, and are 85a, c easily confused with contemporary two-feathers amulets which are made from the same materials and have a similar outline. Possession

86 *Snake heads for protection.*
a) Green-blue glazed-composition snake head with the body extended on a base. LP. b) Cornelian snake head inscribed for the vizier Khay. L. 6.1 cm, 19th Dynasty, (Ramesses II), *c.* 1250 BC. c) Red jasper head with hood markings delineated. NK.
d) Cornelian, with the head at an angle to the body. Saite.
e) Bright turquoise-blue glazed-composition snake head. LP.

of a *pesesh-kef* amulet would guarantee for eternity the deceased's use of all his faculties in the Afterlife.

The object in the shape of a **snake's head**, called variously *mḳrt* (*meqret*), *mnḳryt* (*menqeryt*) and *mnḳbyt* (*menqebyt*), appears as early as the Middle Kingdom in the frieze of items depicted inside non-royal coffins. It first occurs as an amulet in the Eighteenth Dynasty in the burials of King Tuthmosis IV and Tutankhamun and of Yuya and Tjuya, Akhenaten's grandparents; it continued to be found in a royal context in the Nineteenth Dynasty in the Apis burial ascribed to Prince Khaemwese and in the Third Intermediate Period in the burials at Tanis of Psusennes I, Amenemope, Osorkon II and Prince Hornakht. However, snake-head amulets from non-royal 63 burials of the Eighteenth and Nineteenth dynasties are also known: the viziers Aper-el and Khay, who served under Akhenaten and Ramesses II respectively, each owned one.

By far the most popular materials for snakes' heads were red-coloured, whether cornelian, jasper, glazed composition or glass, though 43b gold examples are known. Usually the head and much of the deflated hood are represented with clearly marked eyes, sometimes inlaid, and well-defined ribbing on the neck. During the 86d Late Period, however, a smaller, less-detailed type usually depicts the raised head forming a sharp angle to the neck and resembles more the snake-headed sceptre which this object may originally have represented. The form of the name *menqebyt* perhaps links this amulet with the words for 'fan' and 'coolness', both suggesting that it may have been intended to provide cool refreshment to the throat of the deceased. Otherwise, it may have been worn to ward off snake bites which were as greatly feared by the dead as by the living: Chapter 34 of the *Book of the Dead* had this very aim. Curiously, some bear an address to the eye or uraeus of the sun-god which is also found on *sweret*-beads (see page 99).

The **two fingers** amulet, which represents the index and middle fingers, usually with nails 64h and joints clearly defined, is always made of a 73e dark stone such as basalt, obsidian or steatite, or else of black glass, and occurs only in Late Period burials. Its frequent location on the torso near the embalming incision has led to the suggestion that it represents the two fingers of the embalmer. It would thus have been intended to reconfirm the embalming process or perhaps give added protection to the most vulnerable part of the mummy.

States and Conditions

Characteristic of burials of the Saite Period and later are two amulets which are almost invariably found together, the **carpenter's set-square** and **plummet** (or plumb-line), which were probably both known in Egyptian under the single name *sbꜣ* (*sebꜣ*). The set- 87c, 88a square takes the form of two often unequal lengths of square-sectioned rod which meet at a right angle. The plummet comprises a set- 87a, 88b, c square with its junction at the top from which hangs a cord ending in a weight; the whole instrument was used to check verticality. As often as not there are no internal details, so the outline resembles a pyramid with feet. Both amulets are most frequently made of dark stone, especially haematite in the case of the set-square, although there are a few examples

87 *Measuring amulets.*
a) Haematite undetailed plummet. L.P. b) Gilded wood wedge-shaped symbol of Maat, perhaps representing a platform. L. 2.8 cm, G-R. c) Haematite set square. L.P.

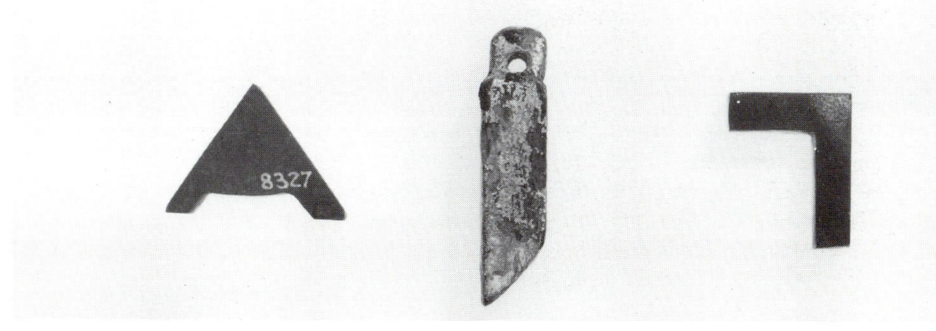

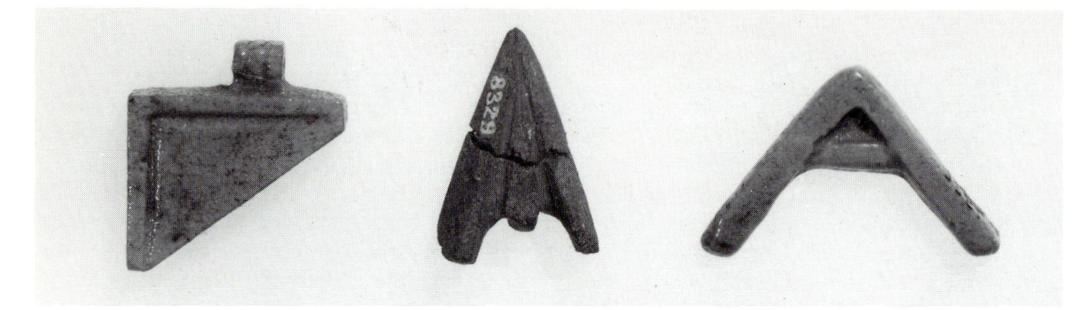

88 *Measuring amulets.*
a) Pale green glazed-composition right angle. LP. b) Dark brown glazed-composition stylised plummet. LP. c) Bright blue glazed-composition plummet. LP.

64d in glazed composition of Ptolemaic date. Possession of a set-square amulet would guarantee its owner everlasting rectitude, a plummet eternal equilibrium.

Amulets in the form of a **writing tablet** are unique to the Twenty-sixth Dynasty and later. They are always rectangular in shape with a suspension tube at the top and made from 99a–c green, blue or dark-coloured material, feldspar being by far the most common. Although the Egyptians used labels in this shape as a writing medium from as early as the First Dynasty, this amulet may well represent rather an undetailed scribe's writing palette which was specifically requested by Chapter 94 of the *Book of the Dead*: 'Bring me a palette from the writing kit of Thoth and the mysteries which are in them.' With such an amulet the deceased would be granted power over whichever magic formula he required in the Other World.

The amulet in the shape of the ***smꜣ*** or ***sma*-** 89c–d **sign** represents an animal's lungs and windpipe which as a hieroglyph writes the word for 'unification' and 'unite'. In appearance it resembles a heart squashed on to a base from which emerges a ribbed shaft with a cross-bar at the top. It is frequently depicted on the sides of the royal throne being tied about with ropes, which end in a papyrus or lily head, knotted tight by the representative gods of Upper and Lower Egypt or the Nile gods of the south and north, the whole scene portraying the unification of the Two Lands. *Sma*-amulets are exclusive to the Twenty-sixth Dynasty and later, and are made from dark-coloured stone – especially obsidian – or, as is common for all funerary amulets of the Late Period, gilded wood. Like the knot-amulet they would guarantee the wearer a unified corpse in the Other World.

Perhaps the best known of all Egyptian amuletic motifs is that called the ***ꜥnḫ*** **(*ankh*)** which, because as a hieroglyphic sign it is used to write the words 'life', 'alive', 'living' and 'to live', embraces all those connotations as an amulet. Although it is constantly depicted carried by royalty and deities, and being offered to their faces, actual individual *ankh* amulets are surprisingly few; the shape is more often found in composite amulets formed from 89e the *djed*, *was* and *ankh* combined, signifying 64o 'stability', 'dominion' and 'life'. The *ankh* or *crux ansata* is formed from a T-shaped cross with an oval loop handle above the cross-bar; the most detailed examples depict binding at the base of the loop. As to what the *ankh* represents pictorially, the most feasible suggestion is that it depicts the tie-straps of a sandal: the loop went around the ankle, the two short arms on either side of the foot and the stem down the foot and between the first and second toes. Another suggestion, however, is that it represents a mirror in its case or even a *tit*-amulet with the flanking folds of material straightened out to form the cross-bar.

The earliest *ankh* amulets date to the late Old Kingdom, and thereafter they occur sporadically throughout the dynastic period, but never in great numbers. Most of the earliest examples are of gold or electrum. Some of the finest, of cornelian, turquoise and lapis lazuli, currently strung into an amuletic necklace, were found in the burial of the Twelfth Dynasty Princess Khnumet at Dahshur. Later, green-glazed composition, the colour of new 89a

89 *Amulets of power.*
a) Pale turquoise-blue glazed-composition flat-backed *tits* and *ankhs*, with loops at the top and bottom, strung as jewellery. Also strung with them are drop-shaped pendants, flat backed *wedjat*-eyes and beads of blue and green glazed composition and cornelian. 18th Dynasty, from Gurob.
b) Turquoise-blue glazed-composition flat-backed *nefer* with a loop at the top and bottom, a jewellery element. NK. c) and d) Steatite *sma* amulets, the first with base support. LP. e) Bright turquoise- blue glazed-composition double-faced *ankh* combined with a *was*. H. 3.3 cm, NK. f) Turquoise-blue glazed-composition staircase. Saite.

7b life and regeneration, became the dominant material.

89b The *nefer*-sign, which resembles a long-necked musical instrument like a lute but actually depicts an animal's heart and windpipe, as a hieroglyph writes words such as 'good', 'beautiful' and 'happy'. In amuletic form, however, its occurrence is strictly limited to being a jewellery element in collars. *Nefers* are made from virtually only hollow gold with moulded top and flat back, occasionally inlaid, or from green-glazed composition. They are particularly common in openwork collars of Eighteenth Dynasty date: a splendid selection of gold examples, gradated in size, many of them inlaid with semi-precious stones, came from the burial of the wives of Tuthmosis III; another group originated from pit 55 in the Valley of the Kings. In spite of its restricted survival, the *nefer* was one of the prescribed

90 *Cosmic elements.* From LEFT to RIGHT
a) Turquoise-blue glazed-composition two sided full moon and crescent. NK. b) Turquoise-blue glazed-composition sun-in-horizon. Saite. c) Red glass sun disc on a plinth. LP. d) Olivine sun disc. LP. e) Red glazed-composition sun-in-horizon. H. 1.4 cm; LP. f) Cornelian openwork flat-backed divine barque, containing full and crescent moons. NK. g) Bright turquoise-blue glazed-composition flat-backed openwork divine barque, containing a seated falcon-headed sun god in disc, flanked by adoring baboons. L. 4.1 cm, late NK.

amulets represented and named in the MacGregor Papyrus list.

It is possible that some other forms which exist as jewellery elements depicting **fruit**, **flowers** and parts of **plants** may also have an amuletic significance. Characteristic of the Eighteenth Dynasty and made almost exclusively of flat-backed multicoloured glazed composition with a suspension loop at the top and sometimes at the bottom too, they were strung to form openwork broad collars. Particularly common are mandrake fruits, lotus and poppy petals, date-palm leaves, daisies, cornflowers, rosettes, lotus and lily heads, bunches of grapes, thistles, palmettes and, less frequently, multiple jasmine flowers. X-rays have revealed that Kha's wife Merit wears a particularly interesting arrangement including, apparently, cos lettuces, the emblem of the fertility god Min. Contemporary examples of all these forms also exist in gold, occasionally inlaid with semi-precious stones and glass. Queen Aahhotep's burial contained a number of hollow gold lotus heads and sheet-gold leaf shapes, that of the wives of Tuthmosis III hollow gold palmettes, and that in pit 55 in the Valley of the Kings hollow gold dates. Hollow gold mandrake fruits, closed lotus buds, lotus seed vessels and papyrus flower heads are also known. All growing plants were inherently symbolic of new life, but some flowers also open each morning, reconfirming the idea of resurrection; grapes were perhaps representative of wine and its regenerative qualities.

65

The amulet in the shape of a **staircase** which resembles a right-angled triangle with the steps running up the long hypotenuse is probably a stylised representation of the primordial mound that first arose out of the waters of chaos and upon which all creation began. The concept of such a mound may well have underlain the first step pyramid: the *Pyramid Texts* tell of a staircase to heaven by which the king might ascend. Later the throne of Osiris as judge of the dead came to be set at the top of a stepped dais. Thus a staircase amulet would have offered the wearer at one and the same time the opportunity for re-creation, resurrection and ascent to heaven. The form is exclusive to the Saite Period and later, and made of blue- or green-glazed composition.

89f

Ḥḥ (*heh*), literally 'infinity' and the related concept 'millions', was originally one of the four male frog demiurges worshipped at Hermopolis with four female snake counterparts as creators of the world. As an amulet he was represented as a kneeling man in profile, his face frontal, with outstretched arms holding in each hand a palm rib (symbolising 'year'), the flopped-over top of each rib meeting on top of his head to give a double hump outline. The whole formed a pictorial message wishing the owner 'millions of years' of life in the Other 4e World. *Heh* amulets occur as early as the late Old Kingdom and are a feature of burials of the First Intermediate Period and Middle Kingdom; thereafter they apparently disappear 16a until the Roman Period. They are most com- 69a monly made in openwork precious metal, especially gold, and often have finely incised detail. At the same time, however, there are examples in openwork glazed composition which are identifiable virtually only by the outline shape, so crude is their appearance.

The burials of the Twelfth Dynasty great ladies Khnumet, Sithathoriunet, Sitḥathor and Mereret were rich in gold amuletic **motto clasps** inlaid with lapis lazuli, cornelian and turquoise, and also with glazed composition, which probably hung on the chest like a pendant. Their inlaid hieroglyphs spell out pious wishes or make statements which would be of use to the dead as well as the living. The commonest messages are 'All life and protection', 'The heart of the two gods is content' – a reference to the conciliation of Horus and Seth – and 'Joy'.

Cosmic Powers

Certain cosmic elements connected with an Afterlife to which originally only pharaoh would have had access were turned into amuletic form during the archaising Saite Period. The **sun disc** in the form of a large 90c, d flattened circle on a small low stand, which sometimes has concave sides, is unique to the Twenty-sixth Dynasty and later; it is made in particular from lapis lazuli or dark-coloured stone like serpentine and basalt and sometimes from a green material such as olivine. With possession of this amulet the deceased could expect to be united with the sun god during his passage across the sky and through the Underworld to be reborn each morning. It is often found near the stomach of mummies.

The **sun-in-the-horizon** amulet, in Egyptian *ꜣḫty* (*akhty*), represents the two hills of the 90b, e eastern horizon with the sun rising between them. Examples are mostly made from red material, jasper, cornelian and red sandstone being by far the commonest with some glass, although green- or blue-glazed composition and schist also occur. This amulet, which is characteristic of the Twenty-sixth Dynasty and later, again links the deceased with rebirth in the company of the newly risen sun.

During the late New Kingdom some very fine raised-relief amulets in bright-blue-glazed composition were made in an open-backed mould depicting a baboon standing with arms

91 *Saite double-animal amulets.*
a) TOP Two complete couchant lions, back-to-back in brown glazed composition. L. 4.1 cm. b) Pale turquoise-blue glazed-composition bulls' foreparts lying back-to-back with a full moon and crescent between. c) Pale turquoise-blue glazed-composition rams' foreparts again placed back-to-back with a full moon and crescent between.

90g raised in adoration at the prow and stern of a **celestial barque** in which sits a falcon-headed sun god with the sun disc on his head. Suspension is by a loop on top of the disc. Baboons were closely connected with the rising sun, whose approach they were believed to anticipate by their cries and upright posture. Clearly, then, this form of amulet has the same purpose as that of the rising sun.

Interestingly enough, another amulet occurs at the same time which is identical save for one important detail: the sun god's figure in the barque is replaced by a crescent with full moon. The baboons are still there because they were connected with the moon too, being the animal manifestation of the moon god Thoth. Sometimes, though, especially when this amulet is made from a hard stone such as 90f cornelian, the baboons are not represented. Individual amulets depicting the **moon with** 90a **crescent**, in which the suspension loop is on top of the crescent so that the piece would hang upside down, are known as early as the Amarna Period and are a feature of the New Kingdom. The medium is almost always green-blue-glazed composition with a few examples in precious metal. Undoubtedly this amulet was intended to link the owner with the ideas of renewal and regeneration inherent in the symbolism of the waning and waxing of the moon.

The vanishing of the stars at dawn and their reappearance at night had obvious symbolism of rebirth after death, but amulets in their form with five rays are known from only three specific periods. The Twelfth Dynasty Princess Khnumet at Dahshur owned two magnificent examples of gold granulation, the centres and outlines edged with gold wire. A contemporary example from a private burial is of glazed composition. This was also the material for star amulets found at Amarna of late Eighteenth Dynasty date and Ptolemaic examples from burials at Dendera which lay at the throat and stomach.

A series of amulets takes the form of two animals' foreparts joined back to back: double lions, bulls, rams and a combination of lion and bull are all found but do not seem to be mere 91 variants of each other. The **double lion**, which occurs as early as the Sixth Dynasty, made from ivory with a flat back, may have rudimentary forepaws or may just represent two lion 4c, heads; examples of this type continued to be produced until the Twelfth Dynasty in cornelian, feldspar and green-glazed steatite. It is not until the Twenty-sixty Dynasty that the form with two complete lion foreparts occurs in the round on a plinth well-modelled from green-glazed composition; even two complete lions back to back are known. Interestingly, 91a this developed type has the suspension loop placed over the animals' back in such a way that it resembles a sun disc, suggesting that there might be an underlying connection with Rwty, the double lion depicted in Chapter 17 of the *Book of the Dead*, over whose back the sun rose each day. Thus an amulet in this form might be intended to link its wearer with daily regeneration in the company of the sun. However, in the MacGregor list the double lion is portrayed and named as *ḫns* (*khenes*). Yet this is a word meaning 'traverse' or 'travel across' which appears in much earlier hieroglyphic texts determined by a sign in the shape of two bulls' foreparts back to back. In fact glazed-composition **double bull** amulets in exactly this form are found in the Twenty-sixth Dynasty and later. To prove the connection between the two types there are even contemporary glazed-composition amulets in which one forepart is a bull's and the other a lion's. Yet double bull amulets are also known which have a full and crescent moon nestling over their backs. More- 91b over, a third form, which first appears in the Third Intermediate Period, represents **double rams**, and in Late Dynastic examples suspen- 91c sion is by a loop behind so that a full moon with crescent can lie over the animals' backs. Presumably by the Late Period the Egyptians themselves had become thoroughly confused by the double animals' symbolism, though for those with the moon there was obviously a lunar connection linking the wearer with that heavenly body's regenerative qualities.

7

Amulets of Offerings, Possessions and Property

Petrie termed ktematic, from the Greek word for 'property', amulets in the shape of possessions which could act as magical substitutes for real clothing, personal accoutrements, goods and equipment taken to the tomb for use in the Other Life which might be stolen or destroyed. The objects represented might be items used in life, but some were of a ritual or funerary nature, made specifically to be set on or near the mummy on the day of the burial. As such, amulets in their shape would always have an underlying symbolism allowing them to be classified just as easily under Petrie's dynatic category as amulets of power. The present attribution must, therefore, be arbitrary. Also included in this category are amulets which might depict funerary offerings, intended to keep the various spirit forms which survived death eternally supplied with essential food and drink even if actual supplies had ceased to be presented at the burial place. Surprisingly, only one amulet can definitely be placed in this category; all the others might have a different symbolism.

Funerary Offerings

92c A fat **trussed ox**, its legs tightly bound beneath its body, carved in the round from red jasper, red sandstone or cornelian, or modelled from red-glazed composition or glass, occurs as early as the Eighteenth Dynasty but has been found *in situ* only on the torso of mummies of the Late Dynastic Period. Composition examples are often found in New Kingdom foundation deposits – caches of miniature tools, samples of building materials and food offerings both real and substitute which were buried beneath or near new building projects. This amulet represented at one and the same time meat as foodstuff and the source of the foreleg, one of the most potent of ritual objects. During the Opening of the Mouth ceremony at the door of the tomb on the day of burial, the foreleg or ***khepesh*** is always shown being presented to the mummy, having just been cut from a still-bleating and still-bleeding calf (which perhaps explains the almost exclusively red colouring, the same as life's blood). Amulets in the shape of the *khepesh* itself (invariably of variously coloured glazed composition) have never been found in a funerary context, only in foundation deposits or perhaps as an inlay hieroglyphic sign. Amulets in the shape of an **ox-head** with open mouth and projecting tongue presumably had the same function as the complete ox, the part representing the whole. However, since ox-heads are often depicted among foodstuffs heaped on offering tables they may well have been considered a choice titbit in their own right. Nevertheless, thus far no amulets in this shape have been found in a funerary context, only in foundation deposits or at manufacturing sites. Ox-headed as opposed to bovine-head amulets (see page 61), are always made from multicoloured glazed composition in open-backed moulds. Finely modelled glazed-composition amulets of a **trussed antelope** (or oryx), probably of New Kingdom date, may also represent food offerings. 92g 92a

As early as the late Old Kingdom amulets were carved in the shape of a **duckling** – the hieroglyphic *ṯ3* (*tja*) – with open beak and 4h

92 *Food offerings and property*. From the TOP, LEFT to RIGHT a) Pale turquoise-blue glazed-composition trussed antelope. 18th Dynasty. b) Dark blue glass obelisk. Ptolemaic. c) Red jasper trussed ox. NK. d) Bright blue glass sandal sole, a substitute for the whole sandal. L. 3.4 cm; Ptolemaic. e) Turquoise-blue glazed-composition amuletic *shabti* funerary figure carrying two hoes. H. 4.1 cm, NK. f) Grey glazed-composition spouted offering table with relief jug and loaf. LP. g) White glazed-composition ox's foreleg, the *khepesh*. 18th Dynasty. h) Alabaster mirror. Roman.

spread wings, nearly always of ivory or bone, some noticeably larger than others. Presumably they represented a food offering, for duck is depicted among foodstuffs for the dead in tombs from as early as the Old Kingdom and actual bones have been found in predynastic settlements. However, all examples are pierced from front to back surface for suspension, which suggests that they were intended to be worn in life; perhaps the fledgling was symbolic of youthfulness. 60b Duck amulets, which first occur in the Eighteenth Dynasty, made in the round from materials as varied as red jasper, cornelian, steatite, glazed composition, 54d glass and gold, are of two kinds. In one the head of the bird is twisted right back to rest on its wings, a posture which implies that it is dead and serving as a food offering, exactly like the ducks carved and painted in offering scenes on tomb and temple walls. It has also been suggested, however, that sleep is depicted and the bird symbolises the promise of reawakening and resurrection. Gold duck amulets are also depicted among awards given at the jubilee of 43b Amenophis III. Examples exist made from hollow sheet gold moulded in two halves with chased details of eye, beak and wing-and-tail feathers. There are 'spots' on the underbellies. The second type depicts either a single bird or a pair side by side, usually in the round. Again, they might represent a foodstuff, but since ducks are a constantly recurring feature in toilet objects such as cosmetic spoons or mirror handles which take the form of a nubile young maiden clutching a bird to her breast, perhaps an erotic symbolism cannot be discounted. Duck amulets have only been found *in situ* on Late Dynastic mummies, on the upper torso.

The Egyptians' ambivalent attitude towards certain animals is revealed particularly in the way in which they regarded fish. On the one hand, from earliest times these creatures formed a staple part of the diet, even for the dead; on the other hand, most of the varieties which were eaten were also sacred to one deity

93 *Amuletic amphibians.* From LEFT to RIGHT
a) Discoloured red glass *Schilbe*, with inlaid eyes, sacred fish of Mendes. Ptolemaic. b) Finger-ring in turquoise-blue glazed composition, the bezel surmounted by two frogs. NK to TIP. c) Turquoise-blue glazed-composition *Tilapia*, symbolic of regeneration. L. 2.5 cm, NK. d) Grey-blue glazed-composition *Barbus*, the *Lepidotus* sacred to Mehyt. LP. e) Green glazed steatite *Lates*, sacred to Neith. LD. f) *Schilbe* in blue-green glazed composition. LP. g) Plaque with seven crocodiles in pale green glazed composition. W. 4.9 cm, Saite.

or another or else taboo. Fish amulets, there-
93 fore, might be pressed into service to substitute for food offerings. This was certainly their function in New Kingdom foundation deposits and may well have been also when they first appear in burials of the late Old Kingdom and First Intermediate Period. In the former the material is almost exclusively glazed composition; in the latter cornelian is even more popular. Yet they were essentially worn in life to place the wearer under the patronage of a particular deity (as with the *Lates*, *Barbus* and *Schilbe*) or to afford particular protection (as
93a, c with the *batensoda* and *Tilapia*). Of all these
4j only the *Tilapia* had a particularly funerary
54h symbolism, for its presence was believed to guarantee new life.

The most important part of any tomb was the offering place where physical food and drink would in theory be set each day for all eternity so that the spirit forms which survived death, in particular the *ka*, should continue to be maintained in the Afterlife. These daily supplies soon came to be set upon an **offering table** on which was carved or painted their image as a second guarantee if the real foodstuffs were not forthcoming: the representation could by magical means come into three-dimensional being. An amulet in the shape of an offering table would thus guarantee a fully supplied Afterlife, yet, curiously, none can be securely dated before the Third Intermediate Period. Made almost invariably of modelled 92f
glazed composition or bronze – though a few undetailed dark stone examples are known – they are rectangular with a suspension loop at the top edge and a spout at the lower, just as on a real altar, to allow liquid offerings to drain away. Internal details range from stylised markings to represent offerings to well-defined raised-relief circular loaves, conical fancy bread and variously shaped vessels.

It is the bronze examples, however, which show an amazing amount of well-moulded detail. All are Late Dynastic in date, have suspension loops and are small and light 94
enough to have been worn by the mummy, albeit vertically. Not only is there a wealth of detailed modelled drink containers and

94 Bronze spouted offering table with drink containers and food in relief. Around rim are solid-cast kneeling figures of the deceased, seated solar baboons, couchant jackals, standing falcons, obelisks, couchant lions and a frog. The underside is inscribed 'May Isis give life to Nesptah son of Padihor'. L. 9.2 cm, Saite.

foodstuffs in the sunken central area, but a three-dimensional frog always squats over the gutter; a figure of the owner in the round, sometimes shown as often as three times, kneels at the sides; and the rim is crowded with various combinations of three-dimensional obelisks, couchant jackals, standing falcons, seated baboons and couchant lions.

Amuletic **miniature vessels**, usually in the round, have survived from all periods, identical in shape with full-sized containers for water, wine, milk and beer. Examples with long bodies tapering to a point, high shoulders and short neck, made from alabaster, steatite and black limestone, occur as early as the First Dynasty; amphorae for wine, however, of identical shape but handled, made from bronze and spotted glazed composition, are not found before the Graeco-Roman Period. The small globular vessel with short neck and rimmed mouth called the *nw*-pot first occurs in predynastic burials and is generally made from cornelian, but some fine Twelfth Dynasty double examples are of hollow gold or silver with a gold neck. Thirty-one gradated hollow gold vessels with an ovoid body and longer neck are probably contemporary with identical full-sized metal containers of Eighteenth Dynasty date. 'Pilgrim' flasks with flattened circular body, two small hoop handles running from neck to shoulder and a flaring mouth, characteristically in glazed composition, might be contemporary with full-sized pottery examples of New Kingdom date. *Qebh*-vases, representing a water container with a spout, do not perhaps appear before the Saite Period; extant examples are of gilded wood. Certainly a

96c

96a

96d

95 *Headrests.*
a) Made from haematite. L.P. b) Made from steatite. L.P. c) Made from pink limestone. L.D. d) Inscribed with Chapter 166 of the *Book of the Dead* for the Store-house Keeper Iahmes. Haematite. W. 3.9 cm, Saite. e) Made from haematite. Ptolemaic.

little earlier, of Third Intermediate Period date, are amulets of a situla – a ritual metal bucket of milk-churn shape with a long hoop handle attached to two loops on the rim – intended to carry holy water for use in sacred activities. Some are made of copper, others of glazed composition.

96f

A tall water vessel with flared foot, short neck, projecting rim and high shoulders called a **hes-vase** was often used in temple ritual. As a hieroglyph, however, it wrote the word meaning 'praise' or 'favour'. Hence the collection of *hes*-vase amulets of cornelian, feldspar, glazed composition and gilded plaster from the Twelfth Dynasty burial of Senebtisy at one and the same time guaranteed her liquid offerings and divine praise or favour in the Other World. The well-modelled leonine head of **Bes** forms the body of a glazed-composition **fancy vessel** amulet with long neck and tall handle, probably of Saite date. An amulet in the shape of a tall, flaring-sided **unguent vessel**, which as hieroglyph writes the name of the cat goddess Bastet, represented a personal possession and its valuable contents: highly scented fatty material was used like perfume to anoint the body. Examples in lapis lazuli and cornelian are probably as early as the Middle Kingdom in date.

96e

96b

Possessions

Chapter 166 in New Kingdom *Books of the Dead* is a spell for a headrest, *wrs* (*weres*), which the accompanying vignette depicts with a long narrow base from which emerges a relatively tall cylindrical shaft ending in a curved rest sometimes filled by a cushion. Actual headrests of wood, ivory or alabaster, often very elaborate in form, were an essential part of an Egyptian household's sleeping arrangements and were taken to the tomb for use in the Other Life; mummies often lay within the coffin with the head resting on one. An amulet in its shape could, of course, act as a substitute, yet before the later Third Intermediate Period firmly dated **headrest** amulets are found only in royal burials: Tutankhamun owned one of iron, as did Prince Hornakht and King Sheshonq II at Tanis. However, from the Saite Period onwards they are very common indeed, made almost exclusively of haematite or a dark-coloured substitute such as basalt, serpentine, obsidian or diorite. A handful of examples are in green-, blue- or red-glazed composition, colours of regeneration and eminently suitable for this amulet since it was essentially intended magically to raise up the head of the deceased in resurrection, just as the sun god was raised above the eastern horizon each morning. However, Chapter 166 further reveals that it would also prevent the deceased's head being cut off, a much-feared fate against which Chapter 43 was specifically directed. Variant forms of the

68

95

96 *Miniature vessels as amulets.*
a) Flattened two-handled flask in dark green glazed composition. NK. b) Lapis lazuli flat-backed unguent jar. MK. c) Alabaster amphora with pointed base. ED. d) Flat-backed spouted ewer in gilded wood. G-R. e) Pale blue-green glazed-composition Bes-vase. Saite. f) Copper situla. H. 2.7 cm, TIP.

weres amulet have a stepped foot, shorter, broader shaft and an almost-horizontal rest; Ptolemaic examples tend to be block-like.

In spite of the fact that combs were found in predynastic burials, bone or mother-of-pearl amuletic examples with a narrow head and a long handle pierced for suspension are all Roman in date. Mother-of-pearl mirror 92h amulets with a round face and short pierced handle are no earlier.

The identification of an amulet unique to private burials of the Late Dynastic and Graeco-Roman Period, which appears to guarantee **clothing** to the deceased, has been much discussed. It resembles a particular type of 97b, h hoop-shaped counterpoise with fringed edge called a *mʿnḫt* (*menkhet*): this is what it is called in the MacGregor Papyrus list. There may be a pun on the word *menkhet* meaning 'clothing', although this is written differently in hieroglyphs. However, from the New Kingdom onwards an apparently identical shape with the 97c sound-value *ʿpr* (*aper*) is used to write words meaning 'equipped' or 'furnished with' and, by extension, 'equipment'; perhaps it actually represents an elaborate apron. The preferred materials are dark stones such as diorite, quartzite or porphyry, but examples exist in gilded wood, gold and glass.

The simple broad collar, *wsẖ* (*wesekh*), formed from multiple strings of beads brought together at each side in a terminal, was worn in life and placed on the mummy, but in the Saite Period it was also taken to the tomb as an amulet, being one of the six collars named and depicted in the MacGregor amulet list. A deep narrow form, representing the collar held 97d bunched rather than worn, occurs in moulded 66e glass or glazed composition, incised or inlaid gold and carved and gilded wood. The prescribed funerary forms, however, intended to afford particular protection, depict an extended collar. Chapters 157 and 158 of the *Book of the Dead* are concerned with prescribed collars in the shape of a golden vulture and of a falcon, both of which were found full-sized on the mummy of Tutankhamun, each once in sheet gold and once in flexible gold cloisonné-work. Already by the Twenty-first Dynasty at Tanis they were being produced in miniature amuletic form for King Psusennes, cut from sheet gold with the wings curved around and all-in-one with the counterpoise. The burials of Prince Hornakht, General Wendjebauendjed and King Amenemope at the same site contained more conventional sheet-gold miniature vulture and falcon collars with outstretched wings, and by the Twenty-

97 *Amulets representing jewellery.*
a) Stamped gold foil broad collar with falcon-head terminals. LD. b) Gilded wood *menkhet* counterpoise. G-R. c) Gilded wood *aper*(?). G-R. d) Sagging broad collar in gilded wood. G-R. e) Grey-blue glazed-composition pylon-shaped pectoral. LP. f) Yellow jasper broad collar with falcon-head terminals on both faces. W. 4 cm; LD. g) Turquoise-blue glazed-composition pendulum-shaped counterpoise. TIP. h) Serpentine *menkhet* counterpoise. LP.

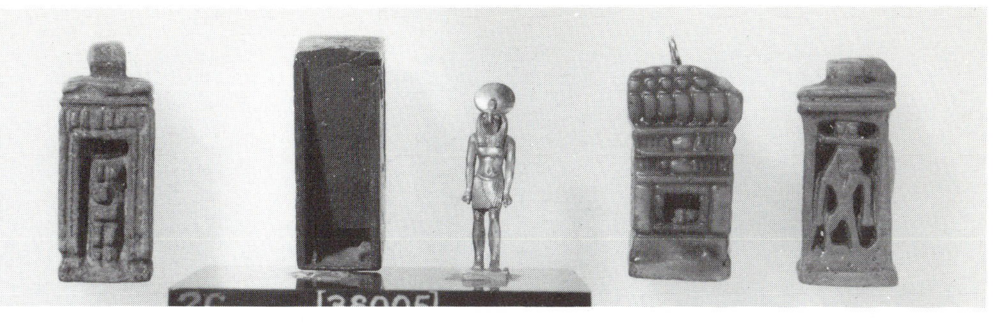

98 *Shrine-shaped amulets.*
a) Pale turquoise-blue glazed-composition shrine containing a seated cat. The sides are decorated with papyrus columns. H. 3.1 cm, TIP. b) Silver shrine and the gold falcon-headed god it contained wearing a disc and uraeus. H. of shrine 3 cm, LP, from Tell Defenna. c) Blue-green glazed-steatite openwork shrine with a bust of the lunar falcon at each side and another in the round within. TIP. d) Grey-green glazed-composition openwork shrine with a figure of Ptah-Tatenen at the back. The sides have winged cobras, the front a stylised hieroglyph. TIP.

sixth Dynasty this type is found in non-royal burials too. Vignettes of Chapter 158 actually depict not a complete falcon but a broad collar with falcon-headed terminals, and that form of amulet is also found in non-royal burials of the Twenty-sixth Dynasty and later, made from sheet gold or cloisonnéwork, gilded wood or stone. The other funerary collars depicted in the MacGregor amulet list are in the form of a winged cobra and a winged cobra with vulture (*nebty*), both of which occurred full-sized on Tutankhamun's mummy in sheet gold, the *nebty* also in flexible cloisonnéwork. At Tanis, Psusennes was the first to own both of them as sheet-gold amulets, but in non-royal burials of the Twenty-sixth Dynasty and later only the winged-cobra collar amulet is found.

In life magnificent precious-metal shrine-shaped reliquaries were worn containing the statuette of a deity to whom the wearer was especially devoted; fine examples have come from the royal burials at Tanis. Glazed-composition amulets in the shape of tiny **shrines**, almost all incapable of being opened and often too poorly detailed to allow certain identification of the god represented, are obviously substitutes for the real thing. They too probably first occur in the Third Intermediate Period. An unusually fine one is openwork with cavetto cornice and frieze of uraei, seated gods on two sides and a winged scarab at the back. The two-leafed door opens to reveal a smaller doorless shrine with a tiny lion-headed *aegis* of Bastet in its depths. Usually, however, three of the sides show seated gods and divine emblems, and the fourth depicts the figure of the main deity, perhaps the squatting baboon of Thoth, the falcon-head with moon of Khonsu or the anthropoid creator god Ptah-Tatenen with horns and plumes. Some examples are solid and without detail.

Pylon-shaped pectorals, especially of openwork inlaid metal, were a characteristic chest ornament from the Middle Kingdom onwards. During the New Kingdom, however, they also came to be made from solid glazed composition purely for funerary purposes and in particular as a setting for the heart scarab (see page 59). As early as the Third Intermediate Period the funerary form was being imitated in a glazed-composition amulet; Saite burials contain miniature sheet-gold examples.

A **seal** amulet represents the stamp seal bearing its owner's titles and name of a kind used occasionally in the Middle Kingdom – scarab seals were far commoner – to stamp into mud sealings which authenticated documents and proved ownership. For some strange reason it was this form, rather than the contemporary cylinder seal which had just been revived, on which the amulet was based when it was invented in the Saite Period. The basic shape is a truncated square pyramid of varying height, sometimes stepped or with flared sides and with a suspension loop on top. The materials used are generally green or blue – feldspar, glazed composition or lapis lazuli – with basalt and some limestone. When found on mummies, this amulet is sometimes, appropriately, on or at the fingers; otherwise it merely lies over the torso. Although uninscribed, a seal amulet by its very existence guaranteed the survival of the deceased's name for all eternity.

99 ABOVE *Writing tablets and stamp seals.*
a) Gilded wood writing tablet with holes for attachment. G–R. b) Green feldspar writing tablet. H. 2.4 cm, Saite. c) Green feldspar writing tablet with an unintelligible hieroglyphic text on one side. The other shows a relief *wedjat*-eye. LP. d) Limestone uninscribed seal amulet. H. 2 cm, LP. e) Steatite stepped and uninscribed seal amulet. LP. f) Lapis lazuli pyramid-shaped seal amulet, uninscribed. LP.

100 BELOW *Set of amulets from a single burial of the later 18th Dynasty.*
a) Red jasper *tit*, uninscribed. b) Discoloured glazed-composition *djed* inscribed for the Royal Scribe and Steward Iy. H. 7.5 cm. c) Black steatite heart inlaid with ivory and green jasper(?) at the bird's head showing the deceased adoring the *benu* bird. The text on the underside is the beginning of Chapter 30B of the *Book of the Dead*. Titles given are High Steward, Royal Scribe and Steward of the Jubilee Temple. d) Cornelian *sweret* bead with the titles Royal Scribe and Steward.

Preserving the name is also often believed to be the function of an elongated cornelian barrel bead called a *sweret*, which was ideally strung alone or with beads of green material to judge from its depiction in the friezes of objects inside Middle Kingdom coffins. Contemporary mummies and anthropoid coffin lids inset with real beads also reveal that the *sweret* was worn at the neck. This location, the material of which it was invariably made and the fact that some New Kingdom examples bear not only the owner's name but also an address to the eye or uraeus of the sun god also found on snake-head amulets (see page 85), has led to the suggestion that both amulets might have shared a similar function, possibly to avert snake bite in the Other World. In the Third Intermediate Period, at any rate, name beads apparently take the form of a similarly shaped glazed-composition bead, mould-made with a curious jagged-edged back. The *sweret*-bead is named and depicted in the MacGregor Papyrus list and contemporary examples, once more of cornelian, show that it had been revived as an amulet.

100d, 77d

16b

Funerary Property

Shabti funerary figures are small statuettes made from various materials which, in their developed form, depict a mummy carrying agricultural implements and are inscribed with Chapter 6 of the *Book of the Dead*, the so-called *shabti* formula, intended to bring the figure to life to carry out the agricultural tasks required of its owner in the Other World. Already in the New Kingdom tiny uninscribed glazed-steatite *shabtis*, complete with implements and pierced for suspension, occur; some have actually been found strung with other amulets. Other mummiform figures of Late Period date, however, usually made of multicoloured moulded glass and without hands, should perhaps be classified with the mummiform human amulet in the MacGregor list called simply 'wrapped mummy'.

92e

Obelisks do not have to be tall needles of granite erected by kings at the entrances of temples; even in the Old Kingdom the doors to private tombs were sometimes flanked by small soft-stone examples. This practice was revived in the Late Period – contemporary funerary papyrus vignettes depicting the last rites at the tomb now show them as the goal of the funeral procession – so it is unsurprising that amulets in their shape now occur for the first time. The obelisk was a sun stone, the important part being the pyramidal capstone representing the mound in the waters of chaos on which the sun god first appeared, and as a religious motif it appears on shabti boxes and coffins offering the deceased the hope of resurrection with the sun. The amulet is made of dark stone,such as basalt, lapis lazuli or steatite, or of glass and pierced for suspension.

92b

8

Materials and their Symbolism

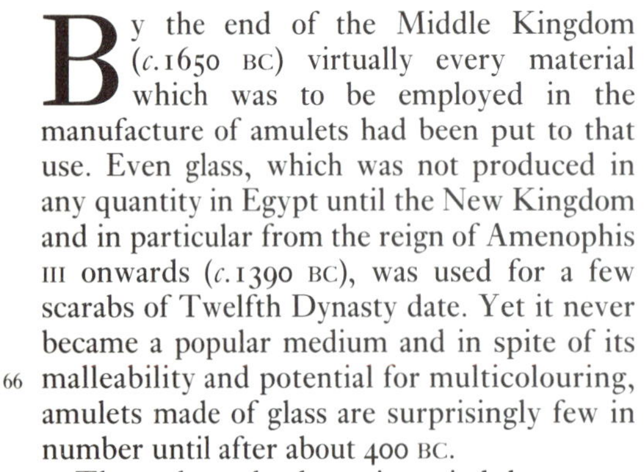

By the end of the Middle Kingdom (*c.* 1650 BC) virtually every material which was to be employed in the manufacture of amulets had been put to that use. Even glass, which was not produced in any quantity in Egypt until the New Kingdom and in particular from the reign of Amenophis III onwards (*c.* 1390 BC), was used for a few scarabs of Twelfth Dynasty date. Yet it never became a popular medium and in spite of its malleability and potential for multicolouring, (66) amulets made of glass are surprisingly few in number until after about 400 BC.

Throughout the dynastic period the material most commonly used in the production of amulets was **glazed composition**, also known less accurately as faience. Perhaps the most characteristic of all ancient Egyptian materials, it consists of a sandy core, ideally but rarely of pure powdered quartz, with a vitreous alkaline glaze on its surface; the glaze can be of any colour, depending on the colourant added to the mixture. (front cover d, 46a) In the Predynastic Period only green and blue glazes occur; black, white and purple are used sporadically from the Old Kingdom onwards and yellow and red were added to the palette during the Eighteenth Dynasty. (39f, 46e, 64a) The reason for the popularity of glazed composition lay in its ability to be moulded (usually in an open-backed pottery mould) or modelled into any amuletic shape. (65, back cover a) While the body material was still soft, a means of suspension was easily supplied by perforation or adding a loop of composition.

Research has suggested that there were three methods by which the all-important surface glazing, essentially a sodium-calcium-silicate or potassium-calcium-silicate, could be achieved and all three were used in the production of amulets. By one method, known as applied glazing, the raw materials in powdered form were mixed with water (a compound known as slurry) and applied to the faience (or stone) body material by dipping, pouring or painting with the result that the glaze formed on the surface during firing. This process is characterised by the unevenness of the resulting glaze which often shows drips, flow lines and a build-up of material in any nook or cranny. Such is the typical appearance of many of the crudely formed glazed-composition amulets found in burials of First Intermediate Period date. This may well have been the earliest method employed by the Egyptians who were glazing steatite, though for beads rather than amulets, even before the beginning of the First Dynasty in 3100 BC. (39c,)

A self-glazing process known as cementation was certainly in use at least as early as the Middle Kingdom. By this method the stone or faience amulet was enveloped in the glazing mixture which might be in a wet or dry state; the mixture melted during firing to form a surface glaze and the excess material could be crumbled away. The third method, another self-glazing process, which could be used to glaze only amulets with a faience body, entailed the mixing of the glazing materials with that of the body. During drying the glazing salts rose to the surface and coated it by a process known as efflorescence; firing melted the surface salts to form the glaze. It must have been one of

101 *Openwork glazed-composition spacer-bars from Third Intermediate Period jewellery.*
From the TOP a) Isis suckles Horus in the delta marshes. There are seven stringing holes in the frame. Light turquoise blue. b) Horus-the-Child carrying a crook, with his finger to his lips, squats on a 'gold' sign flanked by winged cobras. Horus in the Double Crown raises his arm over two prisoners. Light turquoise blue with seven stringing holes in the frame. c) A falcon-headed sun-god, wearing a disc, holds a prisoner. He is flanked by Monthu in double plumes with Mut and Horus in the Double Crown and a lion-headed goddess wearing a disc. There are nine stringing holes. Turquoise-blue. L. 5.5 cm.

these self-glazing methods which produced the rock-hard, uniformly coloured glazed-composition amulets of deities, with amazing sharpness of detail considering the smallness of scale, which are characteristic of the Late Dynastic Period. Glazed composition, invariably green or blue, and to an even greater extent glazed steatite or soap-stone, were the principal materials from which scarabs were made. 44d, e

Egyptian **glass** and the glaze of glazed composition are basically the same material – an alkaline calcium silicate. The difference lies in how they were employed: if the raw product was to form glass, it was used independently; if it was to form glaze, it was provided with a core of a different material. Apart from requiring a far lower temperature for fusion than modern glass, the other main difference is that Egyptian glass was never blown – that process only came into use during the Roman Period – but instead was formed from rods and canes. In the manufacture of amulets the molten material might be modelled in an open pottery mould or mould-pressed, a process whereby a mould was pressed into soft glass which lay against an unyielding surface. Glass amulets might also 66 be pulled into shape at the end of a pontil or cast in a closed mould in the same way as metal. As with composition, while the glass was still soft a means of suspension was supplied by perforation or the addition of a loop of material.

A characteristic glass amulet of late Eighteenth Dynasty date is the heart pulled 66b into shape at the end of a pontil and resembling a pot with knobbed top and lug handles. Whether the body material is black, dark blue, turquoise or sapphire blue, it is always decorated further with trailed threads of white, yellow, green or, more unusually, red. Manufactured in the same way at the end of a pontil are equally colourful amulets which depict 66i Thoeris, hippopotamus goddess of childbirth. Her black body is always decorated with embedded blobs of red and white glass that give a spattered effect very reminiscent in appearance, if not in technique, of composite mosaic glass dishes of the mid- to late Eighteenth Dynasty which are probably contemporary. After about 400 BC the number and range of flat-backed glass amulets increased enormously, but they are generally small, made in worn moulds and not substantially retouched. Virtually the only innovation lies in the use of two or three contrasting colours, each 66h, l, m added separately in a small quantity to fill just part of the mould and allowed to set before the next colour was added. In a slightly different technique, variously coloured strips of glass might be impressed at irregular intervals into the body material.

From the Old Kingdom onwards amulets were sometimes made of **Egyptian blue**, an artificially produced frit consisting of calcium-copper-silicate. Superficially it can be mistaken for glazed composition which has lost its shiny appearance but, unlike composition, where the glaze is only on the surface, the colour is uniform throughout. 64i, m

From earliest times amulets were manufactured from **organic materials** or **animal products**, notably shell, bone and ivory. Whole shells, many from the Red Sea rather than native to the Nile Valley, could in themselves function amuletically, judging from the fact that they came to be imitated in other materials. Even before the beginning of the First Dynasty, bone – whether animal, bird or occasionally fish – was carved into amuletic shapes and this use continued sporadically throughout the dynastic period. Real claws found in predynastic burials were later imitated in semi-precious stones and precious metal, and worn as an element of anklets. Ivory can be obtained from the tusk of elephants and hippopotamuses, but there can be little doubt that it was from the the latter that amulets were shaped during the Predynastic Period: of the two animals only the hippopotamus is represented on contemporary painted pottery, formed into theriomorphic vessels, and gives its shape to slate palettes. From at least the time of the Old Kingdom, however, elephant ivory was imported from Nubia and Punt and during the New Kingdom from Syria too. Nevertheless the primary source for the not inconsiderable numbers of ivory amulets made during the Old Kingdom and First Intermediate Period probably continued to be hippopotamus tusks. Wooden amulets occur rarely and date almost exclusively to the First Intermediate Period, New Kingdom or the Late Period, those of the latter time usually being gilded.

Perhaps surprisingly, it was from difficult-to-work semi-precious stones that many of the earliest recognisable amulets were carved and throughout the Dynastic Period they remained, after glazed composition, the most popular material. Indeed, as early as the Badarian Period steatite or soapstone was glazed green, almost certainly in imitation of feldspar or turquoise. The stones most often carved into amulets are described in the following paragraphs.

Cornelian, a translucent form of chalcedony (silicon dioxide), which ranges in colour from red-brown or orange to a barely red-tinged transparency, is found in considerable quantities in the Eastern Desert and Nubia, yet was considered sufficiently precious to be mentioned in lists alongside silver, lapis lazuli and turquoise. Symbolically cornelian reflects the curious dichotomy which the Egyptians felt to be embodied in the colour red, which was not only connected with blood and hence energy, dynamism and power, but was also linked with the evil-tempered desert-god Seth, patron of disorder, storms and aridity and murderer of his brother Osiris. Thus, in the Late Period, the name for cornelian, *ḥrst* (*herset*), also meant 'sadness'. Amulets of cornelian are known from the Predynastic Period onwards. 64r 45j e, f

Sard, a translucent red-brown variety of chalcedony (silicon dioxide), which is almost indistinguishable from cornelian except for being generally darker in colour, was obtainable from a number of locations in the Eastern Desert. Although sard amulets of Middle Kingdom date are known, its use was otherwise virtually limited to the New Kingdom for scarabs.

Lapis lazuli is an opaque, dark-blue mineral (a sulphur-containing sodium-aluminium-silicate), often streaked with white and flecked with gold impurities, which takes a lustrous polish. The most highly prized of all the Egyptians' semi-precious stones, it was undoubtedly imported at all times, even during the Predynastic Period, almost certainly from Badakhshan in north-east Afghanistan. Symbolically lapis lazuli was the colour of the all-embracing night sky. In the Late Period the principal word for this stone, *ḫsbd* (*khesbed*), was used as a synonym for 'joy' and 'delight'. An amuletic *serekh* bead of lapis lazuli was found in the tomb of the First Dynasty pharaoh Djer at Abydos; tiny lapis lazuli amulets are particularly characteristic of the Late Period. 64g 41a

Turquoise, an opaque, pale sky-blue or blue-green copper-containing basic aluminium phosphate, was obtained alongside copper ore at Wadi Maghara and Serabit el-Khadim in Sinai. Today the best quality turquoise is considered to be the blue type, which is less highly prized when exposure to light has faded it to green, but the Egyptians preferred the green variety, valuing it as the green stone *par excellence* and bracketing it with lapis lazuli in lists of valuable materials. In the Late Period the word for turquoise – *mfk3t* (*mefkat*) – was used as a synonym for 'joy' and 'delight'. In any case green was symbolically the colour of new vegetation, growing crops and fertility, and hence of new life and, by extension, resurrection. Turquoise amuletic *serekh* beads occur in the bracelet found in the tomb of King Djer of the First Dynasty at Abydos.

43a, 46g

Feldspar or **Amazon stone**, an opaque, green or green-blue potassium-aluminium-silicate, is found principally in the Eastern Desert. Another source, worked extensively in ancient times, has been located in the Libyan mountains north of Tibesti on the Tropic of Cancer. Feldspar was one of the six stones considered most precious by the Egyptians and was frequently listed with lapis lazuli and turquoise. Being green, it was symbolic of new life just like turquoise and was the prescribed material for papyrus amulets in accordance with Chapters 159 and 160 of the *Book of the Dead*. Feldspar amulets of Sixth Dynasty date are known.

40b 46l ont er b

Jasper is a hard, often mottled red, green or yellow form of quartz (silicon dioxide). Only the red variety, which is found in a number of localities in the Eastern Desert, and the green type, which occurs naturally alongside or even within layers of red, were generally used in the manufacture of amulets. *Ḥnmt* (*khenmet*), the word for red jasper, was derived from the verb *ḥnm*, 'to delight', and links this stone with the positive aspect of red which was the colour of blood with all its connotations of energy, dynamism, power, even life itself. It was the red stone *par excellence*, prescribed by Chapter 156 of the *Book of the Dead* as the material for the Girdle Tie of Isis amulet. Amulets were made from green jasper as early as the Predynastic Period but it was particularly manufactured into scarabs and especially heart scarabs.

44g ont er c

4c, 45a

Amethyst, a translucent quartz (silicon dioxide) with glassy sheen, can range in colour from a deep violet to a barely violet-tinged transparency. Its chief source during the Middle Kingdom was Wadi el-Hudi south-east of Aswan, although older workings have been found north-west of Abu Simbel. Most amulets and scarabs made from amethyst date to the Middle Kingdom.

44a

Steatite (soapstone), a very soft, easily carved basic magnesium silicate characterised by a greasy or soapy feel (hence its name), ranges in colour from white or grey to black and occurs in a number of locations in the Eastern Desert. The technique of glazing steatite green, practised as early as the Badarian Period, was especially applied later in the manufacture of scarabs, but unglazed amulets are known from the Predynastic Period.

39c, d, 44d

61a

Serpentine is an easily carved opaque to semi-translucent basic magnesium silicate which is often mottled, hence its name of 'snake-like'; it can range in colour from dark green to almost black. Found in a number of locations in the Eastern Desert, serpentine was employed for amulets even before the beginning of the First Dynasty. It was used later in the manufacture of scarabs and in particular heart scarabs.

67d

Limestone is an easily worked opaque calcium carbonate with small admixtures of other materials which cause it to vary widely in quality and to range in colour from cream through yellow and pink to black. The hills which border the Nile from Cairo to Esna are of limestone, but particularly popular for amulets was the black variety found in the Eastern Desert and used as early as the Predynastic Period.

Alabaster in an Egyptian context is a lustrous white or cream calcite (basic calcium carbonate) found in a number of locations in Egypt on the east bank. Being easily carved, it was shaped into amulets even before the beginning of the First Dynasty but its use was very sporadic.

43c

Quartz (milky) is a hard, opaque, white variety of silicon dioxide, two sources for which lay in Nubia, north of Toshka, and a little north of Aswan; it was also imported from Syria. Amulets in this material are known dating to the First Intermediate Period.

back cover c

Rock crystal is a hard, glass-like, transparent colourless quartz (silicon dioxide) found particularly in an area to the west of the Nile Valley between the Faiyum and Baharia Oasis and in Sinai. Although first used in the Predynastic Period for beads, its use for amulets was very restricted.

43c **Chalcedony** is a translucent bluish-white, rather waxy-looking quartz (silicon dioxide) found in a number of locations including the Eastern Desert, Baharia Oasis, the Faiyum, Nubia and Sinai. It was employed for amulets and scarabs from at least the time of the Middle Kingdom.

Chrysoprase is a translucent apple-green variety of chalcedony (silicon dioxide) employed for amulets sporadically between predynastic times and the Roman Period.

Agate is a variety of chalcedony (silicon dioxide), coloured by irregular concentric bands or layers of red or brown, separated by gradations of white to grey. It occurs plentifully in Egypt, usually in pebble form, although at least one source in association with jasper has been identified in the Eastern Desert. Amulets were first produced from it during the Old Kingdom and it continued to be used sporadically throughout the dynastic period.

67g **Olivine** is a translucent, glassy, olive-green (hence its name) magnesium-iron-silicate found in many locations in Egypt. It was shaped into amulets even before the First Dynasty and continued to be employed sporadically during the dynastic period, chiefly for scarabs. A number of pieces formerly identified as beryl have proved subsequently to be olivine.

64h, 61c, 45d **Obsidian** is a translucent, shiny black, naturally formed volcanic glass which was used sporadically for scarabs and especially during the Late Period for specific amulets, notably the Two Fingers. It does not occur in Egypt, its probable source being Ethiopia.

64e **Haematite** is an opaque black or black-grey iron oxide with a metallic sheen which was certainly worked during the Late Period in the Eastern Desert but may have been obtained earlier in Sinai and near Aswan. It came to be employed for specific amulets such as the headrest, the carpenter's plummet and set-square.

Porphyry is the term applied to various igneous rocks which comprise a single-coloured matrix embedded with scattered, differently coloured crystals. A black variety with white crystals, almost certainly obtained from a range of hills near the Red Sea coast, was used for amulets particularly in the Late Period. Another variety containing green crystals with a similar use is from an unidentified source.

64f **Diorite**, a speckled black-and-white igneous rock obtained in the vicinity of Aswan, was used particularly during the Late Period to manufacture funerary amulets.

61e, 44b, **Basalt**, a black or greyish-black igneous rock, often containing tiny glittering particles, occurs in a number of localities within Egypt including the Eastern Desert and in Baharia Oasis and Sinai. It was particularly used for heart scarabs and Late Period amulets.

Schist (more correctly siltstone) is a hard crystalline sedimentary rock coloured in various shades of grey, sometimes with a greenish tint, which occurs in a number of places in the Eastern Desert but especially in the neighbourhood of Wadi Hammamat. Its primary amuletic use was for heart scarabs.

Stone amulets were carved by means of metal-bladed chisels which were at first made of copper, later bronze, tapped when necessary with a wooden mallet. They were invariably drilled for suspension and, as for stone beads, the perforation was by a bow drill, of which sometimes as many as five were operated at the same time if representations are to be trusted. Quartz sand probably served as the abrasive in polishing.

Shortly after the beginning of the First Dynasty amulets were being made in metal: the earliest are probably the **gold** amuletic *serekh* beads in the bracelet from the tomb of King Djer at Abydos which were cast in an open-backed pottery mould. More elaborate metal amulets, however, were manufactured by the *cire perdu* or lost wax method of casting, whereby the object to be cast was first modelled in wax and this matrix covered with a thick mud casing. When it had dried it was pierced, the wax was heated until it melted and was allowed to run off so that it left a closed mould into which the molten metal could be poured. Since the mould had to be broken to extract the casting, the lost wax process did not allow mass-production. One of the earliest amuletic elements made by this process is probably the body of the gold falcon on a necklace found in a Fourth Dynasty grave at Mostagedda. The lost wax method was the most 67a 38a popular for metal amulets made during the last millennium BC, especially those in the shape of deities or sacred animals.

Since the Egyptian craftsman did not have shears or fine saws, separation of the shape in the production of the simplest sheet-metal amulets was achieved by chisel alone punching out around the outline, a technique known as *ajouré*. Internal details might be added by chasing, engraving or repoussé. Chasing is the indentation of details by a blunt-edged chisel tapped by a mallet. An important factor in the use of precious metal, it does not entail any loss of material, which is merely pushed aside. Engraving, on the other hand, involves the gouging out and removal of material; it was not practised on metal to any extent before the later New Kingdom. Repoussé, the complementary technique to chasing, is the working of a design into sheet metal from the back so that the details appear as raised relief on the top surface. Extra clarity can be provided subsequently by chasing into the raised top surface, this time from the front. In both techniques the metal needed to rest against a yielding surface: mud, plaster, wax and resin were all employed. Chasing and repoussé are both exhibited on the gold amulets found in a burial at Nag ed-Deir which dates to the First Dynasty. As is usual, a base-plate was added to each. The finest-quality repoussé work was always produced free-hand using variously shaped punches, but it was quickly realised that if repetition was the aim it was easier to make a stone or metal die into which the design had been previously incised or on which it was already carved in raised relief or even in the round. The gold, shell-shaped amuletic pendants from the Nag ed-Deir burial were certainly made by hammering into a mould.

62a

48d, 43e

69a, 43d

The Egyptians manufactured amulets from virtually every metal available to them, namely gold, electrum, silver, copper and bronze. Even iron was used, albeit rarely, as in the case of the headrest found on the mummy of Tutankhamun.

As has already been seen, amulets were being made from gold as early as the First Dynasty. Almost certainly in the earliest period, the Egyptians obtained the small quantities of the metal they required as tiny nuggets of alluvial gold. Soon improved extraction was achieved by digging up gold-bearing material and washing it, a process known as 'panning', whereby the heavier metal fragments were separated from the lighter matter surrounding them. Eventually, though, it became necessary to mine into hard, gold-bearing quartz to obtain the metal which in ancient times no less than today was synonymous with pharaonic civilisation. For the Egyptians, gold was the material of the flesh of the gods, the colour of divinity. It is found in a number of localities between the Nile Valley and the Red Sea, but was obtained by the Egyptians from three regions in particular, one to the east of Coptos, another to the east of Elkab and the third in Nubia north-east of Wadi Halfa. The earliest workings date to the Old Kingdom.

62, 38, 43, 48, 45h, i

Electrum is both a naturally occurring and an artificially produced compound of which the main constituents are gold and silver. Indeed, since most ancient Egyptian gold is impure, containing by nature various proportions of silver (up to as much as 20 per cent), it is often uncertain whether the metal in question is to be considered electrum or low-grade gold. According to the Egyptians themselves it was obtained from sources located to the south, notably Nubia and Punt. Because electrum is rather harder than gold it was particularly suited to withstand the daily wear and tear imposed on amulets and amuletic jewellery. It was being manufactured into amulets at least as early as the Old Kingdom.

64p, 69a

Silver is found in all ancient gold to a greater or lesser degree; it has even been suggested that most so-called silver objects which predate the Middle Kingdom are actually manufactured from naturally silver-rich gold, which the Egyptians presumably obtained from their gold mines. However, the commonest source of ancient silver, metal-bearing ore, does not occur in Egypt. Consequently, from at least the time of the Middle Kingdom, silver was imported mostly from Asia Minor and so was always more highly prized than gold. Yet silver objects were rather more numerous in Egypt than the pieces which have survived might suggest: unlike gold, silver can corrode away beyond restoration, leaving little trace behind. Symbolically, silver was linked with the moon and was often employed as the material for representations of the lunar disc,

38d, 40e

but rarely for amulets of Thoth or his animal manifestation, the baboon. Although it was always used more sparingly than gold, amulets were made from silver at least as early as the late Old Kingdom.

Copper was the first metal known to the Egyptians and was used as early as the predynastic Badarian Period, though not for amulets: copper amulets do not appear before the Old Kingdom. The addition of tin to 40d copper produces bronze which is not only harder and stronger than the basic metal, but also melts at a lower temperature. However, like copper before it, bronze had only a limited use in the manufacture of amulets until the last millennium BC when small figures of deities and sacred animals made by the lost wax process become characteristic of the period. Although native metal was almost certainly the earliest source, by the Old Kingdom at least, copper was being mined in Sinai and during the New Kingdom it was imported, along with bronze, from Syria, Cyprus and Asia Minor.

102 A detail of a granodiorite statue of king Sesostris III wearing a favourite amulet which has not yet been securely identified. This example resembles a stylised fist holding a pointed implement, others an object wrapped in linen or a linen bag with two knotted tapes (*demedj*). 12th Dynasty (*c.* 1878–1843 BC).

Postscript

The Egyptians made amulets with the intention that their magical powers should last forever. Even for those forms whose primary purpose was to be worn in life, the ultimate resting place was on the mummy in the tomb to be of use in the Afterlife. However, they would surely have been amazed to see members of alien cultures, more than twenty centuries later, living in lands unguessed at, not only still wearing ancient Egyptian amulets such as the *ankh* and scarab for their powers, manufactured thousands of years ago yet surviving until today, but even modern-made replicas of the same forms.

Chronological Table

The names with dates are rulers

PREDYNASTIC PERIOD

Badarian culture (*c.*4500 BC)
Naqada I culture
Naqada II culture (*c.*3200 BC)

EARLY DYNASTIC PERIOD (ED)

Narmer (*c.*3100 BC)
1st Dynasty (*c.*3100–2890 BC)
Djer (*c.*3000 BC)
2nd Dynasty (*c.*2890–2686 BC)

OLD KINGDOM (OK)

3rd Dynasty (*c.*2686–2613 BC)
Djoser (*c.*2650 BC)
4th Dynasty (*c.*2613–2494 BC)
Sneferu (*c.* 2613–2588 BC)
Khufu (*c.*2588–2563 BC)
Khafre (*c.*2553–2528 BC)
Menkaure (*c.*2527–2499 BC)
5th Dynasty (*c.*2494–2345 BC)
Wenis (*c.*2365–2345 BC)
6th Dynasty (*c.*2345–2181 BC)

1ST INTERMEDIATE PERIOD (FIP)

7th-10th Dynasties (*c.*2181–2040 BC)

MIDDLE KINGDOM (MK)

11th Dynasty (*c.*2133–1991 BC)
Mentuhotep II (*c.*2040 BC)
Wah
12th Dynasty (*c.*1991–1786 BC)
Ammenemes I (*c.*1991–1962 BC)
Senebtisy
Ammenemes II (*c.*1929–1895 BC)
Khnumet
Sesostris II (*c.*1897–1878 BC)
Sithathoriunet
Sesostris III (*c.*1878–1843 BC)
Sithathor
Ammenemes III (*c.*1842–1797 BC)
Mereret

2ND INTERMEDIATE PERIOD (SIP)

13th Dynasty (*c.*1786–1663 BC)
Nubhotepti the Child
Sobkhotep IV (*c.*1720 BC)
Nebankh
14th Dynasty (*c.*1715–1650 BC)
15th Dynasty (*c.*1648–1540 BC)
16th Dynasty (*c.*1650–1550 BC)
17th Dynasty (*c.*1650–1550 BC)
Nubkheperre Inyotef VII (*c.* 1650 BC)
Queen Sobkemsaf
Sobkemsaf II (*c.*1590 BC)

NEW KINGDOM (NK)

18th Dynasty (*c.*1550–1295 BC)
Ahmose (*c.*1550–1525 BC)
Queen Aahhotep
Hatshepsut (*c.*1479–1457 BC)
Tuthmosis III (*c.*1479–1425 BC)
Queens Menwi, Merti and Menhet
Amenophis II (*c.*1427–1400 BC)
Sennefer
Tuthmosis IV (*c.*1400–1390 BC)
Amenophis III (*c.*1390–1352 BC)
Yuya and Tjuya
Kha
Akhenaten (*c.*1352–1336 BC)
Aper-el
Tutankhamun (*c.*1336–1327 BC)
RAMESSIDE PERIOD
19th Dynasty (*c.*1295–1186 BC)
Sety I (*c.*1294–1279 BC)
Ramesses II (*c.*1279–1213 BC)
Paser
Khay
20th Dynasty (*c.*1186–1070 BC)
Ramesses III – XI (*c.*1184–1070 BC)

3RD INTERMEDIATE PERIOD (TIP)

21st Dynasty (*c.*1069–945 BC)
Psusennes I (*c.*1039–991 BC)
Wendjebauendjed
Amenemope (*c.*993–984 BC)
22nd Dynasty (*c.*945–715 BC)
Sheshonq II (*c.*890 BC)
Osorkon II (*c.*874–850 BC)
Hornakht
23rd Dynasty (*c.*818–715 BC)
24th Dynasty (*c.*727–715 BC)
25th Dynasty (*c.*747–656 BC)
Shabaka (*c.*716–702 BC)

LATE PERIOD (LP)

Including:

LATE DYNASTIC PERIOD (LD)

26th Dynasty (664–525 BC) (SAITES)
27th–30th Dynasties (525–343 BC)
PERSIAN KINGS (343–332 BC)

GRAECO-ROMAN PERIOD (G-R)

MACEDONIAN KINGS (332–305 BC)
Alexander the Great (332–323 BC)
PTOLEMAIC KINGS
Ptolemy I (305–282 BC)
Ptolemy II–XII (284–51 BC)
Men
Cleopatra VII (51–30 BC)
Queen Amanishakheto (MEROITIC)
ROMAN EMPERORS (30 BC–AD 323)

Bibliography

PETRIE, W. M. F., *Amulets*, (London), 1914
REISNER, G. A., *Amulets (CG)*, I/II, (Cairo), 1907/1958.
MÜLLER-WINKLER, C., *Die Ägyptischen Objekt-Amulette*, (Freiburg), 1987.
SCHLICK-NOLTE, B. and DROSTE zu HÜLSHOFF, V. V., *Liebieghaus-Frankfort am Main, Ägyptische Bildwerke I, Skarabäen, Amulette und Schmuck*, (Melsungen), 1990.

AMULETIC JEWELLERY

ALDRED, C., *Jewels of the Pharaohs*, (London), 1971.
ANDREWS, C. A. R., *Ancient Egyptian Jewellery* (London), 1990.
WILKINSON, A., *Ancient Egyptian Jewellery*, (London), 1971.
VERNIER, E., *Catalogue général des Antiquitées égyptiennes du Musée du Caire: Bijoux et Orfèvreries*, (Cairo), 1927, predates the Tanis discoveries and contains no hint of Tutankhamun's treasures but includes illustrations of groups of amulets found on excavated Late Dynastic mummies.

SCARABS

MARTIN, G. T., *Scarabs, cylinders and other ancient Egyptian seals* (Warminster), 1985, is a comprehensive checklist of publications on the subject, including articles. For the symbolism of the creatures and objects represented see especially Hornung, E. and Staehelin, E., *Skarabäen und andere Siegelamulette aus Basler Sammlungen*, (Mainz), 1976.

EXCAVATION REPORTS

The following publications contain well-dated excavated examples of amuletic forms:

BRUNTON, G., *Matmar*, (London), 1948.
Mostagedda, (London), 1937
Qau and Badari I-III, (London), 1927–8, 1930.
BRUNTON, G. and ENGELBACH, R., *Gurob*, (London), 1927.
ENGELBACH, R., *Harageh*, (London), 1923.
MOND, R. and MAYERS, O. H., *Bucheum* III, (London), 1934.

TUTANKHAMUN'S AMULETS

CARTER, H., *Tomb of Tutankhamen* II, (London), 1927.
REEVES, C. N., *The Complete Tutankhamun*, (London), 1990; its comprehensive bibliography includes those publications in which individual amulets will be illustrated.

APER-EL'S AMULETS

ZIVIE, A., *Découverte à Saqqarah*, (Paris), 1990.

TANIS AMULETS

STIERLIN, H. and ZIEGLER, C., *Tanis, Trésors des Pharaons*, (Freiburg), 1987.
Gold of the Pharaohs, (Edinburgh), 1988, exhibition catalogue.
MONTET, P. 'La nécropole des rois tanite' in *Kemi* IX, 1942, (Paris), deals with a large number of individual amulets in addition to his treatment in the primary publication *La nécropole royale de Tanis* I-III (Paris), 1947–60.

MACGREGOR PAPYRUS LIST

CAPART, J. 'Une liste d'amulettes' in *ZÄS* 45, 1908, (Berlin).

List of object numbers

All numbers are prefixed by EA and refer to objects in the British Museum.

Front cover EA a) 58993; b) 20639; c) 7876; d) 26300.
Back cover EA a) 26311; b) 11638; c) 24395.
Frontispiece EA 64606.
1 Carol Andrews
2 EA 10098, sheet 12.
3 EA a) 63103; b) 59704.
4 EA a) 57710; b) 15425; c) 57773e; d) 52847q; e) 66662; f) 57821; g) 528470; h) 57774k; i) 57774p; j) 52847s; k) 52847h; l) 52847g.
5 EA a) 49336n; b) 63572; c) 57815; d) 57780; e) 57774i; f) 57774a; g) 3288; h) 57785; i) 49336c; j) 57773f.
6 EA a) 60400; b) 24762; c) 71400; d) 64634.
7 EA a) 60468; b) 12213; c) 42164; d) 14540; e) 60533; f) 11673; g) 13719; h) 13713; i) 54918.
8 EA a) 64590; b) 65533; c) 64626.
9 EA a) 11015; b) 59402.
10 EA a) 64633; b) 11641; c) 57866; d) 29096; e) 71025; f) 36455.
11 EA a) 24745; b) 60044; c) 60119; d) 64600; e) 60439.
12 EA a) 60583; b) 52934; c) 11072; d) 64479.
13 EA a) 60736; b) 74096; c) 26745; d) 11252; e) 60037.
14 EA a) 64620; b) 22896; c) 53905.
15 EA a) 54386; b) 65574; c) 18126; d) 61314; e) 60288.
16 EA a) 54332; b) 14380; c) 65331; d) 11076; e) 65520.
17 EA a) 26237; b) 65441; c) 60908.
18 EA a) 66632; b) 66681; c) 11158.
19 EA a) 51811; b) 71026; c) 11314.
20 EA a) 29972; b) 61035; c) 65773; d) 11178; e) 60376; f) 60069; g) 61891.
21 EA a) 61622; b) 11600; c) 36448; d) 64617; e) 11896; f) 36451.
22 EA a) 24748; b) 61199; c) 24761.
23 EA a) 59386; b) 57366; c) 22897.
24 EA a) 61448; b) 61441; c) 62896.
25 EA a) 61819; b) 12021; c) 24738; d) 35405.
26 EA a) 59023; b) 26236; c) 64603; d) 38006; e) 26314.
27 EA a) 64605; b) 24392; c) 51823; d) 64604.
28 EA a) 67387; b) 21931; c) 11965; d) 61897; e) 61811; f) 59859; g) 57902; h) 14758.
29 EA a) 11918; b) 61592; c) 61594; d) 26239.
30 EA a) 64586; b) 11297; c) 60235; d) 66631.
31 EA a) 64611; b) 11864; c) 61409; d) 71024.
32 EA a) 64609; b) 11897.
33 EA a) 11900; b) 56933; c) 36453.
34 EA a) 60203; b) 36454; c) 11821.
35 EA a) 60203; b) 36454; c) 11821.
36 EA a) 67227; b) 63475.
37 EA a) 20655; b) 54488; c) 16214; d) 61217.
38 EA a) 68502; b) 48998; c) 65329; d) 66629; e) 59782; f) 33888; g) 26976; h) 23426, i) 65798.
39 EA a) 11836; b) 64592; c) 22992; d) 57733; e) 64593; f) 65515.
40 EA a) 30049; b) 3360; c) 11057; d) 26307; e) 57903; f) 26231.
41 EA a) 57792; b) 57874; c) 64628; d) 24197; e) 57914; f) 57889.
42 EA a) 24774; b) 30478; c) 30477.
43 EA a) 30484–5; b) 14696; c) 30482–3; d) 3363; e) 59418.
44 EA a) 38073; b) 66816; c) 7922; d) 66814; e) 66817; f) 15517; g) 64378.
45 EA a) 65316; b) 63476; c) 54644; d) 37308; e) 59850; f) 65815; g) 66620; h) 2923; i) 16977; j) 54547.
46 EA a) 29222; b) 14846; c) 12752; d) 13430; e) 90112; f) 16966; g) 15603; h) 7321; i) 29040; j) 15836.
47 EA 7865.
48 EA a) 30486–7; b) 57699–57700; c) 65279; d) 3081; e) 59416–7.
49 EA a) 8411; b) 3084; c) 14587; d) 65332; e) 20646; f) 7499; g) 14586.
50 EA 54244–7.
51 EA a) 64596; b) 64608; c) 11765; d) 61169.
52 EA a) 71027; b) 57334.
53 EA a) 11757; b) 11468; c) 60734; d) 11879.
54 EA a) 48793; b) 46952; c) 53840; d) 66117; e) 69753; f) 66150; g) 59088; h) 45363; i) 32362; j) 40889; k) 48993.
55 EA a) 46781; b) 52970, c) 52810; d) 27870; e) 3648; f) 27170; g) 48908; h) 66112; i) 17829.
56 EA a) 8001; b) 7925; c) 15618.
57 EA a) 35402; b) 15507.
58 EA a) 58992; b) 7124; c) 64659; d) 7120.
59 EA 65090; b) 15548; c) 15544; d) 15528; e) 3441; f) 22577; g) 3475.
60 EA a) 27187; b) 64830; c) 29056; d) 34902; e) 2085; f) 11975.
61 EA a) 15619; b) 8088; c) 8003; d) 66717; e) 26807; f) 29440.
62 EA a) 62460; b) 62494; c) 58600; d) 57592.
63 Carol Andrews.
64 EA a) 57866; b) 3361; c) 57793; d) 8338; e) 8315; f) 59859; g) 64629; h) 59500; i) 64604; j) 14754; k) 14586; l) 65533; m) 71029; n) 30848; o) 65539; p) 65332; q) 7499.
65 EA a) 14790a; b) 5737; c) 7599; d) 67118; e) 7575; f) 67037; g) 67107; h) 67099; i) 57887b; j) 67100; k) 57887a; l) 14790b; m) 14790d; n) 14790c; o) 7559; p) 24037.
66 EA a) 16382; b) 8128; c) 16354; d) 54924; e) 64286; f) 64096; g) 57919; h) 64280; i) 6244; j) 59412; k) 29265; l) 54929; m) 64284.
67 EA a) 62444; b) 57803; c) 57773e; d) 57812; e) 54747; f) 14703; g) 57710.
68 EA 10470, sheet 33.
69 EA a) 3077; b) 24787.
70 EA a) 29054; b) 18066; c) 65134; d) 57701; e) 66178; f) 54743.
71 EA a) 46713; b) 71029; c) 64597; d) 59772.
72 EA a) 65519; b) 3361.
73 EA a) 30035; b) 15717; c) 14862; d) 15718; e) 59500.
74 EA a) 57832; b) 28403; c) 52847; d) 14703; e) 57787; f) 57784; g) 63121; h) 30416.
75 EA a) 2202; b) 23125; c) 7404; d) 8142; e) 27595.
76 EA a) 12035; b) 12059; c) 61973; d) 11612; e) 34266.
77 EA a) 58025; b) 8168; c) 13469; d) 30643.
78 EA a) 11917; b) 14754; c) 57793; d) 59851.
79 EA a) 11925; b) 64610; c) 30460.
80 EA a) 64629; b) 71030; c) 71033.
81 EA a) 8144; b) 54864; c) 54212; d) 15963; e) 13747; f) 2210.
82 EA a) 58141; b) 26977; c) 14708; d) 11303; e) 7509; f) 7431.
83 EA a) 8222; b) 29966; c) 8201; d) 8218; e) 24002.
84 EA a) 64587; b) 48667; c) 12235; d) 60739.
85 EA a) 8161; b) 18095; c) 8164; d) 30848.
86 EA a) 12043; b) 64843; c) 3128; d) 54211; e) 13593.
87 EA a) 8327; b) 2230 c) 8332.
88 EA a) 37392; b) 8329; c) 8338.
89 EA a) 65780; b) 71390; c) 8288; d) 8291; e) 65539; f) 7690.
90 EA a) 18130; b) 7516; c) 8299; d) 6417; e) 8295; f) 22886; g) 66623;
91 EA a) 61499; b) 11938; c) 12016.
92 EA a) 57910; b) 16895; c) 29466; d) 57922; e) 33998; f) 4365; g) 8353; h) 50152.
93 EA a) 16359; b) 65813; c) 29045; d) 15982; e) 57737; f) 61957; g) 17285.
94 EA a) 66672.
95 EA a) 8315; b) 8321; c) 8324; d) 20647; e) 20643.
96 EA a) 7522; b) 18551; c) 32123; d) 2227; e) 11852; f) 23127.
97 EA a) 16980; b) 2238; c) 13381; d) 13334; e) 16965; f) 57904; g) 7511; h) 8177.
98 EA a) 17066; b) 38005; c) 90110; d) 11164.
99 EA a) 2207; b) 8230; c) 8075; d) 6430; e) 23141; f) 54219.
100 EA 50742.
101 EA a) 26233; b) 36071; c) 14556.
102 EA 684.

INDEX

Egyptian Words